# Treasury of
# GOD'S
# VIRTUES

Elaine Wright Colvin

Elaine Creasman

PUBLICATIONS INTERNATIONAL, LTD.

ISBN: 0-7853-3718-0

Library of Congress Catalog Card Number: 98–66092

---

**Elaine Wright Colvin** is director of the Christian Writers Information Network. She is author of numerous articles and poems for a variety of religious magazines and has written several books.

**Elaine Creasman** has written for a variety of publications, including *Guideposts* and *Decision* magazines. She has won several writing awards and has served as the leader of various ministry groups.

# Photo Credits

Front and back cover: **Stephen Studd/Tony Stone Images**

**Sharon Broutzas:** 9, 30, 38, 39, 45, 54, 58, 63, 66, 67, 68, 80, 96, 98, 102, 107, 108, 109, 114, 115, 117, 119, 123, 124, 128, 131, 135, 142, 147, 150, 152, 154, 158, 163, 167, 168, 174, 178, 182, 183, 186, 187, 188, 190, 194, 196, 198, 200, 202, 210, 223, 230, 234, 236, 242, 250, 251, 253, 267, 272, 274, 276, 287, 290, 309, 318, 319; **Ed Cooper:** 75, 118, 127, 130, 132, 136, 140, 143, 155, 159, 161, 172, 173, 257, 271, 277, 289; **FPG International:** William D. Adams: 70; Laurance B. Aiuppy: 106; Ed Braverman: 31; Bruce Byers: 12; Willard Clay: 116, 311; Dennie Cody: 254; Color Box: 13, 32, 72; Jim Cummins: 181; Jeff Divine: 59, 164; Fred Dole: 218; Lee Foster: 207; Eugen Gebhardt: 84; Jeri Gleiter: 204; Dennis Hallinan: 157, 209; Kon Hebert: 243; Jeff Heger: 171; Steve Hix: 11, 199; H. Richard Johnston: 50, 51, 292, 297, 308; Spencer Jones: 145; Shinichi Kanno: 231; Alan Kearney: 44, 65; Kevin Laubacher: 14; Barbara Leslie: 15; D.C. Lowe: 239; Lee Marshall: 232; David McGlynn: 217 (right); E. Nagele: 99, 120, 151, 275, 302; Richard Nowitz: 177; Stan Osolinski: 270; Carolyn Parker: 153; G. Randall: 293; Robert Reiff: 238; J. Robinson: 112; Barry Rosenthal: 19 (top); Ken Ross: 304; Frank Saragnese: 77; A. Schmidecker: 195, 222; Gail Shumway: 19 (bottom), 48, 91; Richard H. Smith: 180; Bruce Stoddard: 52; Bob Taylor: 224; Telegraph Colour Library: 41, 61, 156, 233, 258; Ron Thomas: 34, 122, 213, 214, 216; Arthur Tilley: 74, 260; Larry West: 42, 81; **International Stock:** Wayne Aldridge: 37; Robert Beckhard: 86 (top); Mitch Diamond: 193; Dick Dickinson: 29; Chad Ehlers: 76, 176, 203, 266, 285; Bob Firth: 28, 89, 307; Willie Holdman: 175; Hollenbeck Photography: 279; I.T.P.: 139; Miwako Ikeda: 184, 220; Bob Jacobson: 247; Greg Johnston: 245; Steve Lucas: 55; Zeva Oelbaum: 280; Ron Sanford: 85, 312; Johnny Stockshooter: 219; Paul Thompson: 134; Tom Till: 300; Valder/Tormey: 110, 288; Hilary Wilkes: 303; **Stephen Studd/Tony Stone Images:** Table of contents; **SuperStock:** 18, 20, 21, 25, 26, 33, 36, 43, 46, 47, 49, 53, 56, 62, 69, 78, 82, 83, 87, 88, 90, 92, 93, 94, 97, 103, 104, 105, 111, 113, 125, 126, 138, 141, 144, 146, 160, 162, 166, 169, 179, 185, 189, 191, 192, 197, 212, 225, 227, 228, 229, 237, 240, 244, 246, 248, 252, 256, 259, 261, 263, 264, 273, 281, 282, 296, 301, 305, 310, 314, 315, 316, 317, 320; Christie's Images: 27, 221, 294; Musee d'Orsay, Paris/ET Archive, London: 24; National Gallery, London/Bridgeman Art Library, London: 286; Charles Neal: 208.

Additional photography by Sacco Production/Chicago; Brian Warling

# Acknowledgements

Publications International, Ltd., has made every effort to locate the owners of all copyrighted material to obtain permission to use the selections that appear in this book. Any errors or omissions are unintentional; corrections, if necessary, will be made in future editions.

Page 15: "Pass It On," lyrics by Kurt Kaiser, copyright © 1969 Bud John Songs, Inc. All rights reserved. Used by permission.

Page 17: Taken from A TOUCH OF HIS LOVE by Charles Stanley. Copyright © 1994 by Charles F. Stanley. Used by permission of Zondervan Publishing House.

Page 19: Fran Caffey Sandin, *See You Later, Jeffrey*, Wheaton, Illlinois: Tyndale House Publishers, 1988. Out of print. Permission granted by author.

Page 20: From *Plain Prayers in a Complicated World* by Avery Brooke; copyright © 1975 (Reader's Digest Press), 1993 (Cowley Publications, Boston); by permission.

Page 22: From *Teenagers Pray*. Copyright © 1955 Concordia Publishing House. Used with permission.

Page 30: From *Give Happiness a Chance*, by Phil Bosmans. Used with permission from the author.

Page 31: From *Sitting by My Laughing Fire...*, by Ruth Graham Bell, 1977. Used with permission from the author.

Page 47: Taken from GROWING STRONG IN THE SEASONS OF LIFE by Charles Swindoll. Copyright © 1983 by Charles R. Swindoll, Inc. Used by permission of Zondervan Publishing House.

Pages 50–51: Taken from GROWING STRONG IN THE SEASONS OF LIFE by Charles Swindoll. Copyright © 1983 by Charles R. Swindoll, Inc. Used by permission of Zondervan Publishing House.

Page 54: This material is taken from *My Utmost for His Highest* by Oswald Chambers. Copyright © 1935 by Dodd Mead & Co., renewed copyright © 1963 by the Oswald Chambers Publications Assn. Ltd., and is used by permission of Discovery House Publishers, Box 3566, Grand Rapids, MI 49501. All rights reserved.

Page 57: From *Beyond Our Selves* by Catherine Marshall, Chosen Books, a division of Baker Book House Company, 1961. Used by permission.

Page 62: From *She Wanted to Read* by Ella Kaiser Carruth. Copyright © 1966 by Abingdon Press. Used by permission.

Page 67: Taken from JONI by Joni Eareckson and Joe Musser. Copyright © 1976 by Joni Eareckson and Joe Musser. Used by permission of Zondervan Publishing House.

Page 68: Taken from A TOUCH OF HIS LOVE by Charles Stanley. Copyright © 1994 by Charles F. Stanley. Used by permission of Zondervan Publishing House.

Pages 70–71: Excerpt from THE LIVING FAITH by Lloyd C. Douglas. Copyright © 1955, renewed 1983 by Betty Douglas Wilson and Virginia Douglas Dawson. Reprinted by permission of Houghton Mifflin Company. All rights reserved.

Page 82: From *Spiritual Harvest* by Mary Lou Carney. Copyright © 1987 by Abingdon Press. Used by permission.

Page 87: This material is taken from *My Utmost for His Highest* by Oswald Chambers. Copyright © 1935 by Dodd Mead & Co., renewed copyright © 1963 by the Oswald Chambers Publications Assn. Ltd., and is used by permission of Discovery House Publishers, Box 3566, Grand Rapids, MI 49501. All rights reserved.

Pages 90–91: Excerpt from *A Way Through the Wilderness* by Jamie Buckingham. Copyright © 1986. Used with permission from Jacqueline L. Buckingham.

Page 91: Excerpt from *The Trouble With Being Human*, by Eugene Kennedy, 1986, 1976. Used with permission from Eugene Kennedy.

Pages 94–95: From *Spiritual Harvest* by Mary Lou Carney. Copyright © 1987 by Abingdon Press. Used by permission.

Page 98: Excerpt from *Honesty, Morality & Conscience*, by Jerry White, 1979, 1986. Revised and republished 1996. Used by permission of NavPress/Pinon Press and of Jerry White. All rights reserved.

Page 110: Excerpt from *Honesty, Morality & Conscience*, by Jerry White, 1979, 1986. Revised and republished 1996. Used by permission of NavPress/Pinon Press and of Jerry White. All rights reserved.

Page 114: "Forgiveness" by Lucille Gardner, 1913–1989, with permission from Stella Brown.

Page 116: Excerpt from *Mere Christianity* by C.S. Lewis, copyright © 1943. Used with permission by HarperCollins Publishers, Ltd.

# Acknowledgements, continued

Pages 120–121: Taken from THE BOOK OF GOD FOR CHILDREN by Walter Wangerin, Jr. Copyright © 1981, 1987 by Richard Jacobs & Company. Used by permission of Zondervan Publishing House.

Page 123: Material from *What Works When Life Doesn't*, ChariotVictor Publishing, copyright © 1976. Used by permission of Chariot Victor Publishing.

Page 124: Excerpts from *Something More*, by Catherine Marshall, 1974. Used with permission by Chosen Books, a division of Baker Book House Company, 1961.

Page 130: Taken from *Friends & Friendship*, Jerry and Mary White, NavPress, 1982. Used by permission.

Page 131: Taken from THE QUEST FOR CHARACTER by Charles Swindoll. Copyright © 1982 by Charles R. Swindoll, Inc. Used by permission of Zondervan Publishing House.

Page 135: Quin Sherrer with Ruthanne Garlock, *How to Forgive Your Children*, (Lynwood, WA: Aglow Publications, 1989), 25, 207–8. Used by permission of authors.

Page 136: Taken from *Friends & Friendship*, Jerry and Mary White, NavPress, 1982. Used by permission.

Page 137: Excerpt from *The Bible: A New Translation* by James Moffatt. Copyright 1935 by Harper & Brothers. Copyright © renewed 1962 by James H.R. Moffatt. Reprinted by permission of HarperCollins Publishers, Inc.

Page 146: Excerpt from *Mere Christianity* by C.S. Lewis, copyright © 1943, 1945, 1952. Used with permission by HarperCollins Publishers, Ltd.

Page 147: Excerpt from *The Trouble With Being Human*, by Eugene Kennedy, 1986, 1976. Used with permission from Eugene Kennedy.

Page 147: Excerpt from *See You at the House* by Bob Benson, copyright © 1986 by Bob Benson. Reprinted by permission.

Pages 156–157: Taken from *The ABC's of Wisdom*, by Ray Pritchard. Copyright © 1997 Ray Pritchard, Moody Press. Used by permission.

Page 157: Excerpt from *Honesty, Morality & Conscience*, by Jerry White, 1979, 1986. Revised and republished 1996. Used by permission of NavPress/Pinon Press and of Jerry White. All rights reserved.

Page 159: Excerpt from *What Makes a Man?* by Bill McCartney, Copyright © 1992. Used by permission of NavPress/Pinon Press. All rights reserved.

Page 160: Excerpts reprinted by permission of Girl Scouts of the United States of America. Used by permission.

Pages 162–163: by Mary Jo Melone, copyright *St. Petersburg Times* 1997. Used by permission.

Page 170: *Seven Promises of a Promise Keeper* edited and published by Focus on the Family. Copyright © 1994, Promise Keepers. All rights reserved. International copyright secured. Used by permission.

Page 176: Excerpt from THE LIVING FAITH by Lloyd C. Douglas. Copyright © 1955, renewed 1983 by Betty Douglas Wilson and Virginia Douglas Dawson. Reprinted by permission of Houghton Mifflin Company. All rights reserved.

Page 177: Excerpt from *All the Days* by Vance Havner. Copyright © 1976 by Fleming H. Revell Company, a division of Baker Book House.

Page 181: From *Plain Prayers in a Complicated World* by Avery Brooke; copyright © 1975 (Reader's Digest Press), 1993 (Cowley Publications, Boston); by permission.

Page 190: From *Give Happiness a Chance*, by Phil Bosmans. Used with permission from the author.

Page 191: From *Sitting by My Laughing Fire...*, by Ruth Graham Bell, 1977. Used with permission from the author.

Page 194: Excerpt from *A Man Called Peter* by Catherine Marshall, Chosen Books, a division of Baker Book House Company, 1951. Used by permission.

Page 215: Excerpted from *Out of Solitude* by Henri J.M. Nouwen. Copyright © 1974 by Ave Maria Press, Notre Dame, IN 46556. Used with permission of the publisher.

Page 234: Excerpt from *Florence Nightingale* by Philippa Stewart, 1973, used with permission from Wayland Publishers.

Page 236: Excerpt from *From The Father's Heart* by Charles & Paula Slagle, 1989, used with permission from Destiny Image.

# Contents

# The Pursuit of Virtues

Americans spend millions, maybe even billions of dollars a year on the pursuit of outer beauty. The purchase of plastic surgery, hair transplants, expensive clothes, make-up, hair care, nail care, and exercise machines are all done to help us look our best on the outside. In this race for physical perfection, the pursuit of inner beauty can often be pushed aside. *Treasury of God's Virtues* seeks to embrace the pursuit and celebration of inner beauty, which radiates outward and passes true beauty and joy along to others.

In a world where crime is continually reported and the evil side of human nature is often the focus, reading *Treasury of God's Virtues* will be a pleasant alternative and an uplifting experience. This is a book that celebrates the goodness in people and examines those qualities that make a person virtuous.

We all know people who are virtuous—good, righteous, pure of heart, people of high character. There are religious terms to describe this type of person; we might call them "holy" or "a saint." We might say of such a person, "she is so good," or "he is a blessing," or we might even say, "she has been like an angel to me." That is the wonderful thing about virtuous people—they affect all those they come in contact with.

There is a lot of talk about values and virtues today. According to Kenneth L. Woodward, "'Values' is a morally neutral term that merely indicates preference.... A virtue, by contrast, is a quality of character by which individuals habitually recognize and *do* the right thing" (*Newsweek*, "What is Virtue?" June 13, 1994).

In order to look at the many aspects of the different virtues in an organized way and to more easily discover the nature of true virtue, this book is divided into fourteen chapters, each covering one virtue. The chapters and the contents of each chapter have been, for the most part, arranged in an arbitrary fashion.

The virtues covered in this book overlap one another, and you will find that virtues work together in a person's life. Henry Drummond has said, "Character is unity, and all the virtues must advance together to make the perfect man" (*The Greatest Thing in the World*). There are, of course, additional qualities that could be considered aspects of these virtues, but those included here will at least provide a starting point for those character traits you will want to teach to your children or your grandchildren. You will no doubt also find yourself integrating these virtues more fully into your own life.

The pursuit of virtues—which some have called a matter of developing good habits or making right choices or resisting temptation—is something that can be taken on by anyone. We don't have to be beautiful or rich or famous to become more virtuous. And the path to more virtuous living leads to increased happiness and fulfillment. The pursuit of tangible and temporary pleasures, like possessions or position, leaves us feeling unsatisfied and craving for more. But going after the intangibles, which is the goal of a virtuous life, brings satisfaction and lasting benefits that not only affect us and the people around us, but our offspring for generations to come. "There is but one pursuit in life which it is in the power of all to follow, and of all to attain. It is subject to no disappointments, since he that perseveres makes every difficulty an advancement, and every conquest a victory; and this is the pursuit of virtue" (Colton).

In reading this book, you will note that some of the people mentioned faced great adversity in building character and becoming more virtuous. We hope that this will give you hope during your hard times and an understanding that the right choices made during those times are the building blocks of character and virtuous living.

You will also discover as you read this book that no matter when in history or where in the world a virtue is displayed, virtues are never-changing. A person of faith in 17th-century Germany will have the same qualities as a person of faith in 20th-century America. The diverse personalities included in this book, from different walks of life, places in history, and places in the world, illuminate the universality and timelessness of virtuous living.

As you read of the men and women in this book, what you will notice about them is their goodness of heart, which is an important aspect of virtues. Jesus said, "A good man out of the good treasure of his heart brings forth good things" (Matthew 12:35, NKJV). May these good things presented here be an inspiration to you.

This book is not meant to be read from cover to cover. It can be opened up to any page just as the treasures in a treasure chest can be picked up arbitrarily and enjoyed. So enjoy! Feast your eyes, your mind, and your heart on the treasures found in this book. It is our hope that *Treasury of God's Virtues* will bring many hours of reading pleasure and also be a challenge to your life. May you discover what Alexander Pope has so aptly said, "Virtue alone is Happiness below" ("An Essay on Man").

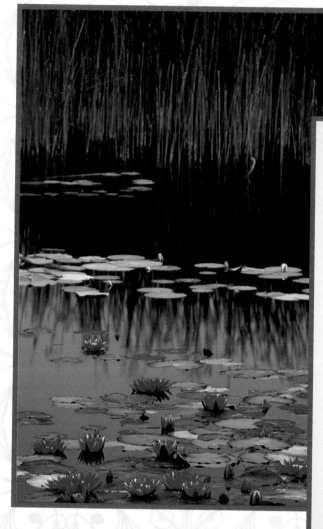

# Love

*God's greatest attribute is love. Love describes who God is and how He feels about us — that He desires to be with us and have an eternal union with us. God commands that we love Him and one another. It is through loving Him that we discover how much we are loved by Him, and then we are able to pass that love on to others. Love is the soul's greatest need, and even our health is better when we know we are loved. Love brings security and calms us. Every other virtue has love at its foundation.*

## God Is Love

*If God has touched us with His love, the result will be love flowing through us to others. When we realize the depth of His love, our hearts long to show that kind of love to those around us.*

Dear friends, let us practice loving each other, for love comes from God and those who are loving and kind show that they are the children of God, and that they are getting to know him better. But if a person isn't loving and kind, it shows that he doesn't know God—for God is love. God showed how much he loved us by sending His only Son into this wicked world to bring to us eternal life through his death . . . Dear friends, since God loved us as much as that, we surely ought to love each other too. For though we have never yet seen God, when we love each other God lives in us and his love within us grows ever stronger.

1 JOHN 4:7–10, 12 (TLB), *HOLY BIBLE*

## Faith Connects Us to Love

*God gives us faith as a means of getting in touch with His love. For once we have that love, we can pass it on to others.*

Love is greater than faith, because the end is greater than the means. What is the use of having faith? It is to connect the soul to God. And what is the object of connecting man with God? That he may become like God. But God is Love. Hence, Faith, the means, is in order to Love, the end. Love, therefore, obviously is greater than faith. "If I have all faith, so as to remove mountains, but have not love, I am nothing."

HENRY DRUMMOND,
*THE GREATEST THING IN THE WORLD* (1891)

## God's Promise of Eternal Love

*God's love is a sure thing that is always reaching out to us. This promise is cause for celebration.*

For I am convinced that nothing can ever separate us from his love. Death can't, and life can't. The angels won't, and all the powers of hell itself cannot keep God's love away. Our fears for today, our worries about tomorrow, or where we are—high above the sky, or in the deepest ocean—nothing will ever be able to separate us from the love of God demonstrated by our Lord Jesus Christ when he died for us.

ROMANS 8:38–39 (TLB), *HOLY BIBLE*

## God's Desire for Love

*God's desire for love from us is not primarily for His benefit, but for ours. One of His deepest desires is that we know His love, and somehow when we take action to love Him, it is then we discover just how much He loves us.*

God wants us to love Him,
not because He is greedy for love,
but because when we are devoted
to loving Him,
we get in touch with
His powerful,
everlasting
love for us.
When we do,
we cannot contain it,
and it overflows to others.

## Drawing Near to God for Love

*We sometimes fear drawing close to God, who is the source of love. Yet, when we finally choose to draw near, what a wonderful discovery we make—we are loved completely.*

For years
I was afraid
To approach You—
afraid You'd disapprove of me
or declare me "unacceptable."

When I finally sought You,
I discovered You were tender,
compassionate, loving.
Now instead of fear,
during my life's purest moments,
I feel secure,
embraced,
totally accepted—
and completely loved by You.

## Passing on God's Love

*God does not love us so that we can hoard His love for ourselves. He desires that we pass it on to others. By spreading the joy of His love, we improve the lives of those around us—and our own lives in the process.*

### Pass It On

It only takes a spark to get a fire going,
And soon all those around can warm up to its
    glowing;
That's how it is with God's love, once you've
    experienced it:
You spread His love to ev'ryone, you want to
    pass it on.

What a wondrous time is spring—when all the
    trees are budding,
The birds begin to sing, the flowers start their
    blooming;
That's how it is with God's love, once you've
    experienced it:
You want to sing, it's fresh like spring, you
    want to pass it on.

I wish for you, my friend, this happiness that
    I've found—
You can depend on Him, it matters not where
    you're bound;
I'll shout it from the mountain top, I want my
    world to know:
The Lord of love has come to me, I want to
    pass it on.

KURT KAISER (1969)

*Love one another, as I have loved you.*

JOHN 15:12 (KJV), *HOLY BIBLE*

## Love Is Most Important

*If we want to determine a list of our accomplishments, we need to put at the top of the list:"What is the quality of love in my life?" That's what God uses to measure our lives.*

If I speak with the eloquence of men and of angels, but have no love, I become no more than blaring brass or crashing cymbal. If I have the gift of foretelling the future and hold in my mind not only all human knowledge but the very secrets of God, and if I also have that absolute faith which can move mountains, but have no love, I amount to nothing at all. If I dispose of all that I possess, yes, even if I give my own body to be burned, but have no love, I achieve precisely nothing.

This love of which I speak is slow to lose patience—it looks for a way of being constructive. It is not possessive: it is neither anxious to impress nor does it cherish inflated ideas of its own importance.

Love has good manners and does not pursue selfish advantage. It is not touchy. It does not keep account of evil or gloat over the wickedness of other people. On the contrary, it is glad with all good men when truth prevails.

Love knows no limit to its endurance, no end to its trust, no fading of its hope; it can outlast anything. It is, in fact, the one thing that still stands when all else has fallen.

For if there are prophecies they will be fulfilled and done with, if there are "tongues" the need for them will disappear, if there is knowledge it will be swallowed up in truth. For our knowledge is always incomplete and our prophecy is always incomplete, and when the complete comes, that is the end of the incomplete.

When I was a little child I talked and felt and thought like a little child. Now that I am a man my childish speech and feeling and thought have no further significance for me.

At present we are men looking at puzzling reflections in a mirror. The time will come when we shall see reality whole and face to face! At present all I know is a little fraction of the truth, but the time will come when I shall know it as fully as God now knows me!

In this life we have three great lasting qualities—faith, hope and love. But the greatest of them is love.

1 Corinthians 13:1–13 (Phillips), *Holy Bible*

## The Facets of Love

*Love is not a warm, fuzzy feeling. It is an attitude and a decision of the heart to put another person's interests above our own. God's love is far above mere human love— it never fails.*

The greatest thing in the world is love. Nothing rivals its power to heal, restore, mend, and make all things new. Love surpasses all other virtues. Set into Scripture like a crown jewel, the thirteenth chapter of First Corinthians shimmers with practical purity of love.

Love is "patient." It is never in a rush, never forceful, never demanding. It waits for God's best, whenever and whatever that may be. It refuses to yield to panic or grasp at temporal solutions.

Love is "kind." It acts in the best interest of others. It overlooks offenses. It is extravagant, giving more than what is asked or needed. Love "does not envy, it does not boast, it is not proud." It waits for God to promote and exalt. It credits him for the success and acknowledges the contributions of others. It applauds the gain of another. It does not flaunt or taunt, but bends its knee in humility.

Love is not "rude." It is polite and courteous to all, even to those who are ill-mannered and ill-tempered. Love is not "self-seeking." It does not relentlessly pursue personal perfection, but gives priority to the kingdom of God.

Love "is not easily angered and keeps no record of wrongs." It is not irritated by the behavior of others. It refuses to judge, leaving that to God. It does not keep a mental record of offenses. Love does not delight in evil, but rejoices with the truth. It meets each day with cheer and a smile. It thinks upon good things and is happy in simple obedience to God.

Love "never fails." It lasts. It works for anyone in any circumstance. It sets you free. It is always the right thing to do. When you choose to love, you have chosen God's way.

Measure your love by these attributes. When provoked or tempted, review this chapter and think on its brilliance. Let its truth light your path. If you are overwhelmed by the enormity of love, choose one of its features and commit yourself to its obedience. Continually turn it over in your mind and heart until it is woven into your spirit.

CHARLES STANLEY, *A TOUCH OF HIS LOVE* (1994)

# True Love

*True love is not based on outer appearances. It goes deeper and is a matter of the heart. Sometimes love is tested to see if it is real. It's inspiring when someone passes the test!*

One day when I was in Brooklyn, I saw a young man going along the street without any arms. A friend who was with me, pointed him out, and told me his story. When the war broke out he felt it to be his duty to enlist and go to the front. He was engaged to be married, and while in the army letters passed frequently between him and his intended wife. After the battle of the Wilderness the young lady looked anxiously for the accustomed letter. For a little while no letter was received. At last one came in a strange hand. She opened it with trembling fingers, and read these words: "We have fought a terrible

battle. I have been wounded so awfully that I shall never be able to support you. A friend writes this for me. I love you more tenderly than ever, but I release you from your promise. I will not ask you to join your life with the maimed life of mine." That letter was never answered. The next train that left, the young lady was on it. She went to the hospital. She found out the number of his cot, and she went down the aisle, between the long rows of the wounded men. At last she saw the number, and, hurrying to his side, she threw her arms around his neck and said: "I'll not desert you. I'll take care of you." He did not resist her love. They were married, and there is no happier couple than this one.

DWIGHT L. MOODY (1837–1899),
*ANECDOTES AND ILLUSTRATIONS OF DWIGHT L. MOODY*

*Many waters cannot quench the flame of love, neither can the floods drown it.*

SONG OF SOLOMON 8:7 (TLB), *HOLY BIBLE*

## Love Letter

*When loved ones are separated by distance or death, the heart grieves. Love letters help bridge the gap and make us feel a little closer to the ones we have lost. But they are only lost for now, not forever.*

Dear Jeffrey,
There was something special about you from the beginning. I could not explain it. Perhaps it was the twinkle in your bright blue eyes or your zest for life. You were with us for such a short time, but Daddy and I loved you very much. We enjoyed every minute. Steve and Angie loved you too. We all miss you and wish you were with us, but the Good Shepherd gathered you into His gentle arms and took you to a better place. As I walk with the Lord each day, I know I am close to you. We'll see you later, Jeffrey. Then, we'll be together forever.

I love you dearly,
Mom

FRAN CAFFEY SANDIN, *SEE YOU LATER JEFFREY* (1988)

## Jesus Loves Everyone

Jesus loves the little children
All the children of the world.
Red and yellow, black and white
They are precious in His sight
Jesus loves the little children of the world.

REV. C. H. WOOLSTON

## Loving Our Neighbor

*Fear and lack of understanding can prevent us from loving our neighbor. If we pray for His assistance, God will help us reach out to our neighbor with His love.*

O Christ, when we do not understand our neighbors, nor they us, help us to think more about how we could understand them and less about how they could understand us. May we never let fear keep us from speaking or acting, nor carelessness increase misunderstanding.

AVERY BROOKE, *PLAIN PRAYERS IN A COMPLICATED WORLD* (1993)

## Who Is My Neighbor?

*God's love does not draw lines. It comes with open eyes, open arms, and an open heart. Can we take the risk of loving our neighbor with God's kind of love?*

One day an expert on Moses' laws came to test Jesus' orthodoxy by asking him this question: "Teacher, what does a man need to do to live forever in heaven?"

Jesus replied, "What does Moses' law say about it?"

"It says," he replied, "that you must love the Lord your God with all your heart, and with your soul, and with all your strength, and with all your mind. And you must love your neighbor just as much as you love yourself."

"Right!" Jesus told him. "Do this and you shall live!"

The man wanted to justify (his lack of love for some kinds of people), so he asked, "Which neighbors?"

Jesus replied with an illustration: "A Jew going on a trip from Jerusalem to Jericho was attacked by bandits. They stripped him of his clothes and money and beat him up and left him lying half dead beside the road.

"By chance a Jewish priest came along; and when he saw the man lying there, he crossed to the other side of the road and passed him by. A Jewish Temple-assistant walked over and looked at him lying there, but then went on.

"But a despised Samaritan came along, and when he saw him, he felt deep pity. Kneeling beside him the Samaritan soothed his wounds with medicine and bandaged them. Then he put the man on his donkey and walked along beside him till they came to an inn, where he nursed him through the night. The next day he handed the innkeeper two twenty-dollar bills and told him to take care of the man. 'If his bill runs higher than that,' he said, 'I'll pay the difference the next time I am here.'

"Now which of these three would you say was a neighbor to the bandits' victim?"

The man replied, "The one who showed him pity."

Then Jesus said, "Yes, now go and do the same."

LUKE 10:25–37 (TLB), *HOLY BIBLE*

## A Prayer for Love of Neighbor

*When neighbors don't measure up to our expectations, we can go to God for a change of heart. With His example and assistance, we can love our neighbors as God wants us to.*

Heavenly Father, out of love for me You have sent Jesus to be my Savior. I am thankful for that, and I want to show my love for You by loving my neighbor. Keep me from harming anyone by hand, mouth, heart, or mind. Help me to bear patiently the wrongs that others do to me. Grant me a forgiving heart that I may not try to gain revenge. Let no angry thoughts arise in my mind, and guard my tongue from angry words.

Fill my heart with love for my Savior that I may show love to others by being kind and helpful to them. Help me to be a good example to others, and use my good example to bring them to know Jesus. Guide all my thoughts, words, and actions that all my doings may bring honor and praise to Your name and good to my friends and neighbors. Take us all to heaven in Your own good time.

Grant these blessings for the sake of Jesus. Amen.

*Teenagers Pray* (1955)

*There is no fear in love; but perfect love casts out fear.*

1 John 4:18 (NKJV), *Holy Bible*

## Loving the Unlovable

*We are naturally drawn to beautiful, kind, loving people. Mature love knows how to love those who seem unlovable, those who seem incapable of giving us anything in return for our love. This kind of love is heaven's love.*

It's not hard to love
those who sparkle—
the diamond people
in the world.
The real test of loving
is being able to love
those who are like
pieces of coal—
those diamonds
in the rough
who might get us dirty.
But if we love them
even so—
with enough positive pressure
from love,
one day
they'll be diamonds too!

## Love the Wicked

*God stretches our heart's capacity when He tells us to love our enemies. Loving them proves that we belong to God, for He loves everyone, no matter what they have done.*

Love your enemies! Do good to them! Lend to them! And don't be concerned about the fact that they won't repay. Then your reward from heaven will be very great, and you will truly be acting as sons of God: for he is kind to the unthankful and to those who are very wicked.

LUKE 6:35 (TLB), *HOLY BIBLE*

## Departed Love

*When we grieve for lost loved ones, we grieve for ourselves. Let us celebrate that those who have gone home to Heaven now know the full essence of God's true love.*

One day I was upon my knees, communing with God upon the subject [of my wife's death], and all at once he seemed to say to me, "You love your wife?" "Yes," I said. "Well, did you love her for her own sake, or yourself? If you loved her for her own sake, why do you sorrow that she is with me? Should not her happiness with me, make you rejoice instead of mourn, if you loved her for her own sake? Did you love her," he seemed to say to me, "for my sake? If you loved her for my sake, surely you would not grieve that she is with me. Why do you think of your loss, and lay so much stress upon that instead of thinking of her gain? Can you be sorrowful, when she is so joyful and happy? If you loved her for her own sake, would you not rejoice in her joy, and be happy in her happiness?"

Charles Finney, An Autobiography

## Loving Like Jesus

*Loving like Jesus is not something that happens automatically. It is not something that's easy or natural. It is learned through the trials of life.*

Often I say, "I want to be like Jesus," or "I want to love like Jesus." Part of me believes it can happen easily. God can wave a magic wand of grace over my life, and suddenly I'll be like Jesus. Reality hit the other day when I remembered how Jesus is described in the Bible: "He was despised and rejected by men, a man of sorrows and familiar with suffering" (Isaiah 53:3, NIV). If I truly want to love like Jesus, I must be willing to be despised and rejected, to be subjected to sorrow and suffering. This is training ground for loving like Jesus. Each time I respond with love when someone is unloving toward me, I take one step closer to loving like Jesus.

Recently I did something I believed was loving toward a person in trouble. But another person looking on decided what I had done was evil and unloving, and she made sure she told me so. How dare she tell me I was evil and unloving! I shouted a list of her own faults back to her, and I ridiculed her for her lack of expertise as a judge of my actions. I let her know I thought she was spiritually blind and relationally stupid.

How did I respond to her verdict of "you are unloving?" By being unloving. How did I respond to her determination that what I—and I believe God—called good, she called evil? With evil. I see how far I have to go to love like Jesus. Repeatedly He faced people who told Him the good He did was evil. He never responded in any other way but with love. Sometimes He spoke a truth in return that hurt the listener, but it was always done in a loving way.

Every day I face tests in love. If I respond in love as Jesus would, I pass. If I don't, I fail. Lord, today I ask that you give me enough grace to respond to rejection with love—just like You did.

## Love That Builds Up

*Real love brings out the best in us. It looks beyond our faults and sees what we can become. This poem reflects that nurturing kind of love.*

### Love

I love you,
Not only for what you are,
But for what I am
When I am with you.

I love you,
Not only for what
You have made of yourself,
But for what
You are making of me.

I love you
For the part of me
That you bring out;
I love you
For putting your hand
Into my heaped-up heart
And passing over
All the foolish, weak things
That you can't help
Dimly seeing there.
And for drawing out
Into the light
All the beautiful belongings
That no one else had looked
Quite far enough to find.

I love you because you
Are helping me to make
Of the lumber of my life
Not a tavern
But a temple;
Out of the works
Of my every day
Not a reproach
But a song.

I love you
Because you have done
More than any creed
Could have done
To make me good,
And more than any fate
Could have done
To make me happy.

You have done it
Without a touch,
Without a word,
Without a sign.
You have done it
By being yourself,
Perhaps that is what
Being a friend means,
After all.

ANONYMOUS

## Love and Mercy

*Even though we may call ourselves "loving," often we justify an action by saying, "he deserved that." When someone comes against us with evil and we respond with good, we are showing mercy.*

There is a word that describes the gap between human love and the love of God. That word is mercy. Repeatedly in Scripture there is reference to God's mercy and loving-kindness. The two go together like love and marriage. Someone has said that grace is God giving us what we don't deserve. Mercy is Him withholding what we do deserve. Because of the evil in us, God's law says we deserve death, but because of His great mercy, which was brought to a climax by Jesus' death on the cross, we can have life instead—eternal life. We did nothing to deserve it. It is given to us by an act of His mercy.

When we consider the breakdown of marriages and friendships and every other human relationship, it is because we are trying to give the other person what we believe he or she deserves. You hurt me, and therefore you deserve to be hurt, is our rationale. What our relationships lack is mercy. Human love is how we behave toward someone who is loving toward us. Mercy or divine love is how we behave when someone has been unloving toward us. Mercy is unnatural for human beings. It is natural for God. That is why His love is far greater than ours. Yet as we draw close to Him and desire to be like Him, a miracle can take place in our lives. We can have mercy on others as He has had mercy on us. Imagine the wonders that love and mercy can work if they flow freely through us to every person we come in contact with. Let us never forget the wonders of God's mercy toward us—that is the key to letting it flow to others.

## Through God's Eyes

*When we see our enemies from God's perspective, compassion follows, for He has seen the sorrows in their hearts that have caused them to behave in such a manner. He longs to reach out to these people and comfort them, and He sometimes uses our hands to do it.*

One dark morning when ice was forming a halo around each street lamp, a feeble-minded girl two rows ahead of us soiled herself. A guard rushed at her, swinging her thick leather crop while the girl shrieked in pain and terror. It was always terrible when one of these innocent ones was beaten. Still the *Aufseherin* continued to whip her. It was the guard we had nicknamed "The Snake" because of the shiny dress she wore. I could see it now beneath her long wool cape, glittering in the light of the lamp as she raised her arm. I was grateful when the screaming girl at last lay still on the cinder street.

"Betsie," I whispered when The Snake was far enough away, "what can we do for these people? Afterward I mean. Can't we make a home for them and care for them and love them?"

"Corrie, I pray every day that we are allowed to do this! To show them that love is greater!"

And it wasn't until I was gathering twigs later in the morning that I realized that I had been thinking of the feeble-minded, and Betsie of their persecutors.

Corrie ten Boom, *The Hiding Place* (1971)

*'Tis better to
have loved and lost,
Than never to
have loved at all.*

Lord Tennyson, "In Memoriam"

## To Love Brings Happiness

*We reflect the goodness of God most when
we love others. It is life's highest, and
sometimes most difficult, goal.*

Not long ago we sat by the bedside
of a dying woman who had experienced
every blessing that life had to offer. We
asked her what had made her the happiest. She did not answer that it was husband, children, home, or position. She
replied, "To love."

Alice Bishop Kramer and Albert Ludlow Kramer,
*I Bring You Joy*

## A Loving Friend

Friend, you give so much to me —
a listening ear
a soothing voice
a caring heart
a helping hand
a healing hug
a cheering smile.
Thanks for being a loving friend.

## Love and Friendship

*A healthy friendship enhances our lives. What a blessing to have someone who wants to share all our joys and sorrows. We should continually strive to be the kind of friend God would like us to be—and the kind of friend that we would like to have.*

Love from friendship—this love leads to light,
to peace and to deep joy.
This love never harms people.
It does not possess for itself.
It leaves the other person free.
And when it finds expression
in physical tenderness,
it stays pure.
But when one person wants
to possess another for himself alone,
for his own satisfaction,
he destroys the person he thinks he loves.
And destroys the friendship.
True, you will never be capable
of a totally unselfish friendship.
But you must always keep trying.

PHIL BOSMANS, "LOVE AND FRIENDSHIP,"
*GIVE HAPPINESS A CHANCE* (1980)

*A friend loves at all times.*

PROVERBS 17:17 (NKJV), *HOLY BIBLE*

*Greater love has no man
than this, that a man lay
down his life for his friends.*

JOHN 15:13 (RSV), *HOLY BIBLE*

# Prayer of a New Bride

*The love of a new bride is fresh and exciting toward her husband—this man of her dreams.*
*God will honor the sincere prayer of a bride young or old to keep that love alive.*

Never let it end, God,
never—please—
all this growing loveliness,
all of these
brief moments of
fresh pleasure—
never let it end.
Let us always
be a little
breathless at love's beauty;
never let us
pause to reason
from a sense of duty;
never let us
stop to measure
just how much to give;

never let us
stoop to weigh love;
let us live—
and love!
Please, God,
let our hearts kneel always,
Love their only master,
knowing the warm impulsiveness
of shattered alabaster.*
I know You can see things
the way a new bride sees,
so
never let it end, God,
never—please.

* Mark 14:3

RUTH BELL GRAHAM, FALL 1943,
*SITTING BY MY LAUGHING FIRE*... (PUBLISHED IN 1977)

# Measured By Love

*We do not naturally love like God does, but we can desire to grow in demonstrating His love to others. Our Christian fervor can be measured by our desire to grow in love, in spite of the struggles we will undoubtedly encounter.*

The growth of Christian life is to be measured by the growth of love; and love itself is to be measured in its progressive states by its restfulness, its undisturbed trust, its victory over every form of fear. The state of perfect loving is incompatible with distrust. When the heart is first awakened to affection, it is disturbed and agitated. It fluctuates with every shade of hope and fear alternately. It rushes from one extreme of confidence to the opposite of doubt. But this is only while it is filling. The heart beginning to love is like a bay into which the star-drawn tides are rushing. The waters come with violence. They stir up the sand and sediment. They dash and murmur on the edges of the shore. They whirl and chafe about the rocks, and the whole bay is agitated with strife and counterstrife of swirling waters, until they have nearly reached their height. Then, when great depth is gained, when the shores are full, when no more room is found for the floods, the bay begins to tranquillize itself, to clear its surface; and effacing every wrinkle, and blowing out every bubble, and hushing every ripple along the shore, it looks up with an open and tranquil face into the sky, and reflects clearly the sun and moon that have drawn it thither. And so does the soul, while filling, whirl with disquiet, and fret its edges with wrinkles and eddies; but when it is filled with love, it rests and looks calmly up, and reflects the image of its God.

HENRY WARD BEECHER, *LIFE THOUGHTS* (1858)

## Sometimes Love Means Letting Go

*One of the hardest things about loving someone is when we must*
*helplessly watch them make wrong decisions and learn life's*
*lessons the hard way. Every parent knows the ache of watching*
*the children we love make foolish choices.*

Sometimes love hurts
especially when we see loved ones
heading for danger.
We call to them, "Watch out!"
We grab at them
and try to bring them back
to a safer place.
But they don't listen.
They break loose,
ignoring our warnings.
And we must stand
on safe ground
and let them go
to learn the hard way.
And if our love is enduring,
we stand with open arms
to welcome them back
when they finally decide—
I am finished with danger—
I must go home.
And if our love is true,
we do not hold to,
"I told you so,"
but "I love you—
even so."

## Sacrificial Love

*O. Henry's timeless story is about much more than beautiful hair combs and a platinum fob watch chain. It's about true love's willingness to give everything—even those things that are most treasured—for those we love.*

"Jim, darling," she cried, "don't look at me that way. I had my hair cut off and sold it because I couldn't have lived through Christmas without giving you a present. It'll grow out again—you won't mind, will you? I just had to do it. My hair grows awfully fast. Say 'Merry Christmas!' Jim, and let's be happy. You don't know what a nice—what a beautiful nice gift I've got for you."

"You've cut off your hair?" asked Jim, laboriously, as if he had not arrived at that patent fact yet even after the hardest mental labor.

"Cut it off and sold it," said Della. "Don't you like me just as well, anyhow? I'm me without my hair, ain't I?"

Jim looked about the room curiously.

"You say your hair is gone?" he said, with an air almost of idiocy.

"You needn't look for it," said Della. "It's sold, I tell you—sold and gone, too. It's Christmas even, boy. Be good to me, for it went for you. Maybe the hairs of my head were numbered," she went on with a sudden serious sweetness, "but nobody could count my love for you. Shall I put the chops on, Jim?"

Out of his trance Jim seemed quickly to wake. He enfolded Della . . .

Jim drew a package from his overcoat pocket and threw it upon the table.

"Don't make any mistake, Dell," he said, "about me. I don't think there's anything in the way of a haircut or a shave or a shampoo that could make me like my girl any less. But if you'll unwrap that package you may see why you had me going a while at first."

White fingers and nimble tore at the string and paper. And then an ecstatic scream of joy; and then, alas! a quick feminine change to hysterical tears and wails, necessitating the immediate employment of all the comforting powers of the lord of the flat.

For there lay The Combs—the set of combs, side and back, that Della had worshiped for long in a Broadway window. Beautiful combs, pure tortoise shell, with jeweled rims—just the shade to wear in the beautiful vanished hair. They were expensive combs, she knew, and her heart had simply craved and yearned over them without the least hope of possession. And now, they were hers, but the tresses that should have adorned the coveted adornments were gone.

But she hugged them to her bosom, and at length she was able to look up with dim eyes and a smile and say: "My hair grows so fast, Jim!"

And then Della leaped up like a little singed cat and cried, "Oh, oh!"

Jim had not yet seen his beautiful present. She held it out to him eagerly upon her open palm. The dull precious metal seemed to flash with a reflection of her bright and ardent spirit.

"Isn't it a dandy, Jim? I hunted all over town to find it. You'll have to look at the time a hundred times a day now. Give me your watch. I want to see how it looks on it."

Instead of obeying, Jim tumbled down on the couch and put his hands under the back of his head and smiled.

"Dell," said he, "let's put our Christmas presents away and keep 'em a while. They're too nice to use just at present. I sold the watch to get the money to buy your combs. And now suppose you put the chops on."

The magi, as you know, were wise men—wonderfully wise men—who brought gifts to the Babe in the manger. They invented the art of giving Christmas presents. Being wise, their gifts were no doubt wise ones, possibly bearing the privilege of exchange in case of duplication. And here I have lamely related to you the uneventful chronicle of two foolish children in a flat who most unwisely sacrificed for each other the greatest treasures of their house. But in a last word to the wise of these days let it be said that of all who give gifts these two were the wisest. Of all who give and receive gifts, such as they are wisest. Everywhere they are wisest. They are the magi.

O. HENRY, "THE GIFT OF THE MAGI"

## Love, Marriage, and Romance

*Thinking of our own needs comes naturally. Thinking of what others need is super-natural. Anyone who's been married knows that sensing the needs of our spouse is a skill worth developing.*

We have to give conscious attention to sensing the other person's needs and extending ourself beyond our own needs to meet them. We may not be too good at it at first, but we become more skillful through practice. Love in any marriage whose romance provides excitement and thrills, is an art. Anyone who becomes an artist at anything does so by developing superior skill in performance. Romance would be constantly in our marriage if more of us were skillful in the fine art of love.

W. CLARK ELLZEY, *HOW TO KEEP ROMANCE IN YOUR MARRIAGE* (1954)

# Humility

ost of us realize that we are naturally self-centered, and we often respond to those around us in ways that make us appear proud, haughty, or arrogant. But if we look at Jesus' life, we see an excellent example of humility—an example that we should strive to follow. He taught that pride was destructive, but humility was powerful. Rather than touting His own greatness, Jesus was willing to kneel down and wash the feet of others, to show that we should all be servants to each other—and to God.

*Humility, that low, sweet root*
*From which all heavenly virtues shoot.*

THOMAS MOORE (1779–1852)

## Fullness of Life

Contentment, and indeed usefulness, comes as the infallible result of great acceptances, great humilities—of not trying to make ourselves this or that, but of surrendering ourselves to the fullness of life—of letting life flow through us.

DAVID GRAYSON

*He has shown you, O man, what is good.*
*And what does the Lord require of you?*
*To act justly and to love mercy*
*And to walk humbly with your God.*

MICAH 6:8 (NIV), *HOLY BIBLE*

*But all who humble themselves before the Lord shall be given every blessing, and shall have wonderful peace.*

PSALM 37:11 (TLB), *HOLY BIBLE*

*Clothe yourselves with humility toward one another, for God is opposed to the proud, but gives grace to the humble. Humble yourselves, therefore, under the mighty hand of God, that He may exalt you at the proper time.*

1 PETER 5:5c–6 (NAS), *HOLY BIBLE*

## Understanding Humility

*Like a multi-faceted stone, the humble person's colors shine forth. By their nature, they are able to bear an injustice without retaliating, do one's duty even when one is not watched, keep at the job until it is finished, and make use of criticism without being defeated by it.*

At one time true humility was thought to mean thinking negatively of oneself or belittling oneself. But this is neither a correct interpretation, nor is it a current definition. It is more accurate to look at humility as not thinking more highly of oneself than we ought to think: "Be honest in your estimate of yourselves, measuring your value by how much faith God has given you" (Romans 12:3, NLT).

Humility actually means not thinking of oneself, but putting others first. We disregard our rights and ambitions so we can serve God by serving others. Arriving at a place of humility is a result of understanding the biblical advice to "serve each other with humble spirits, for God gives special blessings to those who are humble, but sets himself against those who are proud. If you humble yourselves under the mighty hand of God, in his good time he will lift you up" (1 Peter 5:5–6, TLB).

The major obstacle to humility is pride. Pride and self-will become hindrances to our life of faith when we believe that either God does not care about or does not understand our situations in life. Or we believe that we don't need God's help to live our Christian life—we think we can look out for ourselves. When pride lures us into living independently of God, the result can be disastrous. The Book of Proverbs is full of warnings about the danger of allowing pride to creep into our lives: "Pride leads to arguments; be humble, take advice and become wise" (Proverbs 13:10, TLB). "Pride ends in destruction; humility ends in honor" (Proverbs 18:12, TLB).

## A Humble Habit

*Sometimes the best way to humble ourselves is just to walk outside and see everything God has created. A daily walk provides a peaceful way to focus on the world outside ourselves.*

It is not always easy to simply step aside into solitude and rest and quietness. But unless I learn how, my entire growth in God will be endangered.

As a simple first step in this direction may I suggest the reader take twenty minutes each day to go out and walk alone—a brisk walk—only smiling to strangers—deliberately looking for the beauty and handiwork of God in the natural world about him, and inwardly adoring the Lord for who He is. Leave the worries and work at home or in the office. It will prove to be a tonic, a rest that results in growth in God.

Most of us have never learned the humble though powerful practice of concentrating on Christ. Outside, walking alone, away from the usual surroundings which remind us of our feverish workaday world, we can give our hearts a chance to center their interest and affection on Him.

W. Phillip Keller, *As A Tree Grows* (1966)

# A Prayer for Humility

*Only a life of prayer can help the believer
arrive at a spirit of humility, meekness, and
Christlikeness.*

I am praying, blessed Savior,
To be more and more like thee;
I am praying that thy Spirit
Like a dove may rest on me.

I am praying, blessed Savior,
For a faith so clear and bright
That its eye will see thy glory
Thro' the deepest, darkest night.

I am praying to be humbled
By the power of grace divine,
To be clothed upon with meekness,
And to have no will but thine.

I am praying, blessed Savior,
And my constant prayer shall be
For a perfect consecration,
That shall make me more like thee.

Chorus:
Thou who knowest all my weakness,
Thou who knowest all my care,
While I plead each precious promise,
Hear, oh, hear and answer prayer.

FANNY J. CROSBY

## The Secret of Rest

*Rather than proudly striving to get ahead on our own, we must learn to relax in the provision God has made for us. Only this will bring us God's peaceful rest.*

Try to see the relation between meekness and restfulness. Many speak of humility as the secret of rest. You will not have rest while you are proud, neither will you have it just because you try your best to be humble. This may make life all the harder. It is only as you come to Jesus that you will find rest, and you will never come to Him as you believe Him proud instead of humble. Pride separates. You must come to Him as the meek and lowly One, believing Him to be such. 'Tis human to be proud; 'tis Godlike to be humble. You must see it in this way. Jesus can rest you because He is meek. Pride causes one to think of self. One has time for thought of others when he has little need of thought of self. Perhaps you have heard that the best way to rid yourself of a burden is to seek to bear another's burden; that to take upon you the yoke of another, means to be rid of your own yoke. But you can do this in a way that will cure your misery or add to it. Another's yoke may be far heavier than yours, and yet bearing it may rest you.

Bearing it may add to your strength, while bearing your own weakens you.

Jesus' yoke and burden is that of others. He cannot have burdens of His own, for He is without pride. Reputation Jesus did not care about, for He made Himself of no reputation. Riches of earth He did not covet, so loss of money could not affect him. He could not be troubled by outward losses; to Him there could not be loss in these. Some care for one thing for self, some for another; He cared for nothing, and so He was care-free. This is noble living. The truly great are the truly meek. They must be so.

DAVID C. COOK, *REST; OR, THE SONG OF LOVE* (1898)

## Jesus Humbled Himself

*Christ was the perfect example of what being humble really means. While it may be difficult, we should make every effort to follow His example of humility.*

Don't be selfish; don't live to make a good impression on others. Be humble, thinking of others as better than yourself. Don't just think about your own affairs, but be interested in others, too, and in what they are doing.

Your attitude should be the kind that was shown us by Jesus Christ, who, though he was God, did not demand and cling to his rights as God, but laid aside his mighty power and glory, taking the disguise of a slave and becoming like men. And he humbled himself even further, going so far as actually to die a criminal's death on a cross.

Yet it was because of this that God raised him up to the heights of heaven and gave him a name which is above every other name, that at the name of Jesus every knee shall bow in heaven and on earth and under the earth, and every tongue shall confess that Jesus Christ is Lord, to the glory of God the Father.

PHILIPPIANS 2:3–11 (TLB), *HOLY BIBLE*

## The Secret of True Humility

The Apostle Paul was deeply humble. He knew he had worked hard and accomplished much, but only because God had poured kindness and grace upon him. True humility is not convincing yourself that you are worthless, but recognizing God's work in you. It is having God's perspective on who you are and acknowledging his grace in developing your abilities.

1 CORINTHIANS 15:9, *LIFE APPLICATION BIBLE NOTES* (TLB)

*Humble yourselves in the sight of the Lord, and he shall lift you up.* James 4:10 (KJV), Holy Bible

*The humble shall see their God at work for them.*
*No wonder they will be so glad!*
*All who seek for God shall live in joy.*

Psalm 69:32 (TLB), *Holy Bible*

# Everyone Makes Mistakes

*The prophet Isaiah reminds us to "look to the rock from which you were hewn, and to the quarry from which you were dug" (Isaiah 51:1, NAS). By recognizing that everyone has to overcome sinful errors, we are less prone to boast proudly of our own achievements.*

Before we get all enamored with our high-and-mighty importance, it's a good idea to take a backward glance at the "hole of the pit" from which Christ lifted us. And let's not just *think* about it; let's admit it. It has a way of keeping us all on the same level—recipients of grace. And don't kid yourself, even those who are extolled and admired have "holes" from which they were dug.

With Moses it was murder.
With Elijah it was deep depression.
With Peter it was public denial.
With Samson it was recurring lust.
With Thomas it was cynical doubting.
With Jacob it was deception.
With Rahab it was prostitution.
With Jephthah it was his illegitimate birth.

Not even that bold body of reformers had lily-white pasts. Why, some of them had crawled out of the deepest, dirtiest, most scandalous "holes" you could imagine. And it was *that* which kept them humble, honest men . . . unwilling to be glorified or idolized. As they took Isaiah's advice and looked at "the hole of the pit," they found no place whatsoever for pride.

CHARLES R. SWINDOLL, *GROWING STRONG IN THE SEASONS OF LIFE* (1983)

*It is better to be of a humble spirit with the lowly,*
*Than to divide the spoil with the proud.*

PROVERBS 16:19 (NAS), *HOLY BIBLE*

## Humility vs. Pride

*There is an appropriate time to have pride in our accomplishments as well as a time to be humble.*

In God's scale of values, humility stands very high. He has always loved to advance the humble. Such a quality should be ever growing.

Paul acknowledged in 1 Corinthians 15:9, "I am the least of the apostles, that am not meet to be called an apostle" (KJV). Another time he was able to boast, "I have fought a good fight" (2 Timothy 4:7). So there is the right kind of pride, but it is always tempered by humility.

TED W. ENGSTROM, *THE MAKING OF A CHRISTIAN LEADER* (1976)

# No More, No Less

*What does humility really mean? It doesn't mean you should look down on yourself, but that you should accept yourself for who you are, including the good and the bad.*

I had long misunderstood humility. Thinking it to be like an inferiority complex, I adopted a properly despondent look and asserted that I was nothing — I couldn't sing, couldn't preach, couldn't play the piano or any other instrument, was barely coordinated enough to walk. People would respond as expected by saying, "My, you are so humble." In all "humility" I would thank them for noticing.

Now, I realize that this attitude was not humility, it was sickness. Humility is no hangdog approach to life. Humility is simply seeing ourselves as we actually are, not higher nor lower. It means being gut-level honest about ourselves — being up front. It means knowing who we are and owning that — and owning our emotions. It means living without hypocrisy.

GAYLE D. ERWIN, *THE JESUS STYLE* (1983)

## Jesus Despised Self-Righteousness

*Beware of smugness and pride—do not let those feelings guide your actions. Instead, try to keep your thoughts and actions genuine, rather than using them to gain attention from others.*

Listen to Matthew 6:1: Beware of practicing your righteousness before men to be noticed by them...

In other words, stop showing off! Stop looking down your nose at others who don't fill your pre-conceived mold. Stop displaying your own goodness. Stop calling attention to your righteousness. Stop lusting to be noticed. Implied in this is the warning to beware of those who refuse to stop such behavior. And then, to blaze that warning into their memories, He went on to give three specific examples of how people show off their own righteousness so that others might ooh and aah over them.

Matthew 6:2 talks about "when you give alms" or when you are involved in acts of charity assisting others in need. He says don't "sound a trumpet" when you do this. Keep it quiet...even a secret (6:4). Don't scream for attention like Tarzan swinging through the jungle. Stay out of the picture, remain anony-mous. Don't expect to have your name plas-tered all over the place. Pharisees *love* to show off their gifts to others. They love to be made over. They love to remind others who did this and that, or gave such and such to so and so. Jesus says: Don't show off when you use your money to help somebody out.

Matthew 6:5 talks about what to do "when you pray." He warns us against being supplicational showoffs who love to stand in prominent places and mouth meaningless mush in order to be seen and heard. Phar-isees love syrupy words and sugar-crusted platitudes. They've got the technique for sounding high-and-holy down pat. Everything they say in their prayers causes listeners to think that this pious soul resides in heaven and was tutored at the feet of Michael the archangel and King James V. You're confident that they haven't had a dirty thought in the past eighteen

years . . . but you're also quietly aware that there's a huge chasm between what is coming out of the showoff's mouth and where your head is right then. Jesus says: Don't show off when you talk with your Father.

Matthew 6:16 talks about what to do "when you fast." Now that's the time the showoff really hits his stride. He works over-time trying to appear humble and sad, hoping to look hungry and exhausted like some freak who just finished crossing the Sahara that afternoon. "Do not be as the hypocrites!" Christ commands. Instead, we ought to look and sound fresh, clean, and completely natural. Why? Because that's real—that's *genuine*—that's what He promises He will *reward*. Jesus says: Don't show off when you miss a couple or three meals.

Let's face it. Jesus spoke with jabbing, harsh words concerning the Pharisees. When it came to narrow legalism or self-righteous showing off, our Lord pulled no punches.

CHARLES R. SWINDOLL,
*GROWING STRONG IN THE SEASONS OF LIFE* (1983)

*True humility and respect for the Lord lead a man to riches, honor and long life.*

PROVERBS 22:4 (TLB), *HOLY BIBLE*

## True Humility

True humility is viewing ourselves as we really are from God's perspective and acting accordingly. People today practice false humility when they talk themselves down so that others will think they are spiritual. False humility is self-centered; true humility is God-centered.

COLOSSIANS 2:18, *LIFE APPLICATION BIBLE NOTES* (TLB)

## Humility Is My Aim

*"So our aim is to please him always in everything we do…" (2 Corinthians 5:9, TLB).*

MY AIM IS…
>    to please Him through communing in prayer
>    to show His love and for others care
>    to read His Word as my guide for life
>    to cease my grumbling that causes strife
>    to be open to God's leading and His will
>    to take time to meditate, be quiet, and still
>    to continually grow in my Christlike walk
>    to be more like Jesus in my life and my talk.

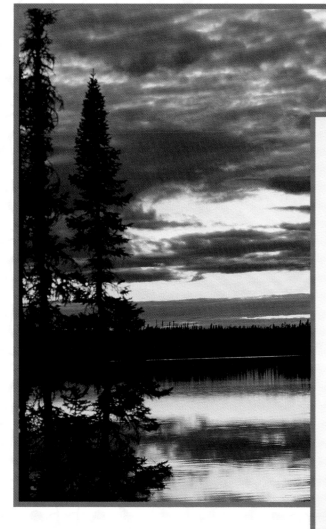

# Faith

To have faith is to believe, to trust, to have confidence in, or to rely on something or someone. Faithfulness describes the quality of someone with unswerving allegiance to an oath or a promise. Our example of faithfulness comes from a God who has kept and is in the process of keeping every promise contained in the Scriptures. We are commanded to "have faith in God," and out of that faith flows our ability to remain faithful to people—to keep the promises we have made as husbands and wives, as children, as parents, and as servants of God.

It is never a question with any of us of faith or no faith; the question always is, "In what or in whom do we put our faith?"

ANONYMOUS

Faith never knows where it is being led, but it loves and knows the One Who is leading.

OSWALD CHAMBERS, *MY UTMOST FOR HIS HIGHEST* (1935)

## The Object of True Faith

*Faith thrives when we stay focused on God rather than on ourselves.*

Faith is the least self-regarding of the virtues. It is by its very nature scarcely conscious of its own existence. Like the eye which sees everything in front of it and never sees itself, faith is occupied with the Object upon which it rests and pays no attention to itself at all. While we are looking at God we do not see ourselves— blessed riddance. The man who has repeated failures will experience real relief when he stops tinkering with his soul and looks away to the perfect One. While he looks at Christ the very things he has so long been trying to do will be getting done within him. It will be God working in him to will and to do.

Faith is not in itself a meritorious act; the merit is in the One toward Whom it is directed. Faith is a redirecting of our sight, a getting out of the focus of our own vision and getting God into focus.

A. W. TOZER, *THE PURSUIT OF GOD*

## Lessons About Faith

*When we attempt to explain our faith to others, it may not help them, but it can assist us in understanding why we believe and what weak spots exist in our faith.*

"Now don't push the term *faith* at me," a lawyer told me bluntly at a dinner party recently. "The word is like a red flag."

"Why such a violent reaction?" I asked.

"Well, because I object to the way Christianity uses faith as a theological gimmick to duck all rational problems. At every point where a man wants to understand, they say, 'You just have to have faith,' or 'Reason can only go so far.' I resent it! I see nothing wrong with 'Prove it to me first, then I'll believe.'"

As we talked, I realized that it had never occurred to this intelligent, well-educated man that in everyday life he often follows the reverse order—belief and acceptance first, then action. Every day he lives, he acts on faith many times with little proof or none at all, and he does not feel that he is being impractical.

He demonstrates an act of faith each time he boards a plane. He believes that it will take him to his destination, but he has no proof of it. He entrusts life itself to several unknown mechanics who have serviced the plane, as well as to a pilot about whom he knows nothing.

Each time he eats a meal in a restaurant he trusts some unknown cook behind the scenes and eats the food on faith, faith that it is not contaminated. He enters a hospital for an operation and signs a release giving permission for surgery. This is an act of faith in an anaesthetist whose name he may not even know and a surgeon who holds in his hands the power of life or death.

He accepts a prescription from a doctor and takes it to a druggist, thus acting his faith that the pharmacist will fill the prescription accurately. The use of the wrong drug might be deadly, but he is not equipped to analyze the contents before swallowing the pill.

It is obvious that were we to insist on the "proof first, then faith" order in our daily lives, organized life as we know it would grind to a screeching halt. And since life together among men is possible only by faith, as we act our trust in other people, it should not seem odd that the same law applies to our life with God.

The New Testament makes it clear that in the spiritual realm, when for some reason or other we refuse to act by faith, all activity stops just as completely as it does in the secular realm. There is no way for us even to take the first steps toward the Christian life except by faith, any more than a baby can get launched on his earthly life without blind baby-trust in his parents and other adults. We have to accept the fact of a personal relationship with Jesus Christ by faith, even as our children accept the fact of parental love. For the child, as for the new Christian, understanding and proof come later.

In the same way, every step in our Christian walk has to be by faith.

In Jesus' ministry of healing the spirit, the mind, and the body, faith seems to have been necessary before the divine act, not (as logic would have it) afterward....

Much of my own problem with faith arose from an early misunderstanding of what faith is. First of all, I used to believe that faith had something to do with feeling. For example, when I had messed up some situation and had asked God for forgiveness, then I would peer inside myself to see if I *felt* forgiven. If I could locate such feelings, then I was sure that God had heard and had forgiven me. Now I know that this is an altogether false test of faith.

We would not be so foolish as to go to a railroad station, board the first car we saw, then sit down and try to feel whether or not this was the train that would take us where we wanted to go. Our feeling would obviously have no bearing on the facts. Yet I know now that at times my actions in the spiritual realm have been just that foolish.

CATHERINE MARSHALL, *BEYOND OUR SELVES* (1979)

## Steps for Growing in Faith

*If we want to grow in faith, we must cooperate with God. Doing our part is the key to growing in faith. Getting to know Him and His ways will enable us to "see" what He is asking us to do.*

For as you know him better, he will give you, through his great power, everything you need for living a truly good life: he even shares his own glory and goodness with us! And by that same mighty power he has given us all the other rich and wonderful blessings he promised; for instance, the promise to save us from the lust and rottenness all around us, and to give us his own character.

But to obtain these gifts, you need more than faith; you must also work hard to be good, and even that is not enough. For then you must learn to know God better and discover what he wants you to do. Next, learn to put aside your own desires so that you will become patient and godly, gladly letting God have his way with you. This will make possible the next step, which is for you to enjoy other people and to like them, and finally you will grow to love them deeply. The more you go in this way, the more you will grow strong spiritually and become fruitful and useful to our Lord Jesus Christ. But anyone who fails to go after these additions to faith is blind indeed, or at least very shortsighted, and has forgotten that God delivered him from the old life of sin so that now he can live a strong, good life for the Lord.

2 PETER 1:3–9 (TLB), *HOLY BIBLE*

*Without faith, we are as stained glass windows in the dark.*

ANONYMOUS

## More Precious Than Gold

*If our faith was never tested, how would we know we had any? When things go wrong and we can still say, "I believe in God no matter what happens," we show our faith to be real.*

These trials are only to test your faith, to see whether or not it is strong and pure. It is being tested as fire tests gold and purifies it—and your faith is far more precious to God than mere gold; so if your faith remains strong after being tried in the test tube of fiery trials, it will bring you much praise and glory and honor on the day of his return.

1 PETER 1:7 (TLB), HOLY BIBLE

## The Testing of Faith

*Faith sometimes means giving back to God the things and people we cherish most. Abraham's faith was tested, and his response has become a model of faith for all believers.*

Later on, God tested Abraham's [faith and obedience].

"Abraham!" God called.

"Yes, Lord?" he replied.

"Take with you your only son—yes, Isaac whom you love so much—and go to the land of Moriah and sacrifice him there as a burnt offering upon one of the mountains which I'll point out to you!"

The next morning Abraham got up early, chopped wood for a fire upon the altar, saddled his donkey, and took with him his son Isaac and two young men who were his servants, and started off to the place where God had told him to go. On the third day of the journey Abraham saw the place in the distance.

"Stay here with the donkey," Abraham told the young men, "and the lad and I will travel yonder and worship, and then come right back."

Abraham placed the wood for the burnt offering upon Isaac's shoulders, while he himself carried the knife and flint for striking a fire. So the two of them went on together.

"Father," Isaac asked, "we have the wood and flint to make the fire, but where is the lamb for the sacrifice?"

"God will see to it, my son," Abraham replied. And they went on.

When they arrived at the place where God had told Abraham to go, he built an altar and placed the wood in order, ready for the fire, and then tied Isaac and laid him on the altar over the wood. And Abraham took the knife and lifted it up to plunge it into his son, to slay him.

At that moment the Angel of God shouted to him from heaven, "Abraham!"

"Yes, Lord!" he answered.

"Lay down the knife; don't hurt the lad in any way," the Angel said, "for I know that God is first in your life—you have not withheld even your beloved son from me."

Then Abraham noticed a ram caught by its horns in a bush. So he took the ram and sacrificed it, instead of his son, as a burnt offering on the altar. Abraham named the place "Jehovah provides"—and it still goes by that name to this day.

Then the Angel of God called again to Abraham from heaven. "I, the Lord, have sworn by myself that because you have obeyed me and have not withheld even your beloved son from me, I will bless you with incredible blessings... all because you have obeyed me."

GENESIS 22:1–18 (TLB), *HOLY BIBLE*

# Obstacles to Faith

*When a task requiring faith confronts us, voices around us may say, "It can't be done." The voice may even come from within us, and we may want to quit before we start. But if we hold on to faith, we can succeed, no matter what the critics say.*

## It Couldn't Be Done

Somebody said that it couldn't be done,
　　But he with a chuckle replied
That "maybe it couldn't" but he would be one
　　Who wouldn't say so till he'd tried.
So he buckled right in with the trace of a grin
　　On his face. If he worried he hid it.
He started to sing as he tackled the thing
　　That couldn't be done, and he did it.

Somebody scoffed: "Oh, you'll never do that;
　　At least no one ever has done it";
But he took off his coat and he took off his hat,
　　And the first thing we knew he'd begun it.
With a lift of his chin and a bit of a grin,
　　Without any doubting or quiddit,
He started to sing as he tackled the thing
　　That couldn't be done, and he did it.

There are thousands to tell you it cannot be done,
　　There are thousands who prophesy failure;
There are thousands to point out to you one
　　　　by one,
　　The dangers that wait to assail you.
But just buckle in with a bit of a grin,
　　Just take off your coat and go to it;
Just start in to sing as you tackle the thing
　　That "cannot be done," and you'll do it.

EDGAR GUEST, *THE PATH TO HOME* (1919)

## Faith Brings Rewards

*Some people blame their lack of faith on their difficult circumstances. Yet rough situations are often the catalyst for displays of great faith.*

*We live by faith, not by sight.* 2 CORINTHIANS 5:7 (NIV), HOLY BIBLE

In 1949 the trustees of Rollins College in Winter Park, Florida, asked Mary to accept an honorary degree.

Mary Bethune received the first honorary degree ever given to a Negro by a white southern college.

She stood as tall as she could as she listened to President Holt say, "Mary McLeod Bethune, I deem it one of the highest privileges that has come to me as President of Rollins College to do honor to you this morning. I am proud that Rollins is, I am told, the first white college in the South to bestow an honorary degree on one of your race. You have in your own person demonstrated that from the humblest beginnings and through the most adverse circumstances it is still possible for one who has the will, the intelligence, the courage, and the never-failing faith in God and in your fellow man to rise from the humblest cabin in the land to a place of honor and influence among the world's eminent . . ."

ELLA KAISER CARRUTH, *SHE WANTED TO READ: THE STORY OF MARY MCLEOD BETHUNE* (1966)

*For the LORD loves the just
and will not forsake his faithful ones.*

PSALM 37:28 (NIV), *HOLY BIBLE*

## A Mother of Faith

*Sometimes a person doesn't have much faith in himself, but a loved one has faith enough to fill in the gaps.*

Who could have believed that the worst student in Higgins Elementary School fifth grade would one day become a world-famous brain surgeon? That a poor ghetto kid would learn to perform operations too risky for some of the most highly trained surgeons to attempt? That the kid who got zero out of thirty on his math quizzes would regularly snatch the lives of tiny children from the edge of death?

Mother believed. She told me many times, "If you ask the Lord for something and believe he will do it, then it'll happen." My life is living proof that it's true.

BEN CARSON, M.D., DIRECTOR OF PEDIATRIC
NEUROSURGERY, JOHN HOPKINS UNIVERSITY, FROM THE
BOOK *BEN CARSON*

## Faith Dreams Big

*In 1976, Millard Fuller and his wife founded Habit for Humanity, which has assisted in building 60,000 homes for low-income families around the world.*

I often say that there is a difference between faith and foolishness. We want to challenge people to get as close to foolishness as they can . . . without crossing the line. Think creatively and boldly! Go ahead and set a date! With God, all things are possible.

MILLARD FULLER, *A SIMPLE, DECENT PLACE TO LIVE* (1995)

# Learning About Faith From Children

*When someone, especially an expert, predicts the worst, we tend to believe them. It takes a dynamic faith to believe something different— to believe that God can and will intervene in the situation. This true story tells of a child who had that kind of faith.*

"Let's pray together for Riffy," I said to my daughter, Tami, who was six years old.

I took our frail cat into my arms and stroked his caramel-colored fur. The doctor had told us there was no hope. The unknown infection, unresponsive to medication, was taking over Riffy's body. His fever remained high, his appetite low. The doctor said we could bring him home, but the symptoms would worsen. Then we could bring him back to be put to sleep.

I prepared in my mind a prayer about helping Tami deal with his inevitable death.

But before I could get my prayer out, Tami began, "Oh God, we know You have great power. Please make Riffy all better, because he is my best friend. Amen."

Now we have a problem, I thought. I tried to say the prayer I had planned about preparing for Riffy's death, but Tami would have none of it.

"God is going to make Riffy well, Mommy," she insisted. "I know He wouldn't take my best friend away from me."

How could I explain to her that God did not always heal? How could I explain God's sovereign plan, which we did not always understand? How could I explain the statement, "If it be Thy will?"

I did not argue with her. I marveled at her faith (or was it naivete?). Worrisome thoughts about what was going to happen when Riffy's condition worsened nagged at me.

"Don't worry, Mom—Riffy will get better soon," she assured me.

Riffy did get well. The day after Tami's prayer, he started eating again. Purring and playing came next, and before long—much to our amazement (my husband's and mine and the doctor's)—Riffy was back to his frisky self again. Once again he hid under Tami's bed to pounce out and bite our toes. He chased rodents in the yard and sometimes generously delivered them to our front door. And he resumed his regular adventure of climbing the tall pine tree in our back yard.

The only one who wasn't amazed by Riffy's recovery was Tami. She'd had faith all along.

## Coping by Faith

*By faithfully turning to God in times of loss and grief, we discover that He can be depended upon to carry us through. Dave Dravecky, a former pitcher for the San Francisco Giants, recounts the loss of his arm to cancer and the faith that got him through the ordeal.*

I'm not getting through the loss of my arm because I am a great coper. I'm getting through it because I have a Father in heaven who is a great giver. He is where I find grace. At the time I need strength, he puts it in my heart or provides it through someone who is close to me, whether that's a family doctor or simply a friend. I don't earn it. I don't deserve it. I don't bring it about. It's a gift.

DAVE AND JAN DRAVECKY, *WHEN YOU CAN'T COME BACK* (1992)

*Now faith is being sure of what we hope for and certain of what we do not see.*

HEBREWS 11:1 (NIV), *HOLY BIBLE*

## Walking on Water

*It's amazing what we can accomplish if we keep
our eyes off our circumstances and on the One
who is in control of them.*

Sometimes I'm like Peter,
and I walk on water.
I stand above my circumstances,
which are like the swirling tempests of the sea.
But then, like Peter,
I take my eyes off Jesus
and concentrate on things below.
Soon I start to sink.
How I long to have
a consistent
water-walking
eyes-on-Jesus
faith.

*I've been driven many
times to my knees by the
overwhelming conviction that
I had nowhere else to go.*

ABRAHAM LINCOLN, *THE WIT & WISDOM OF ABRAHAM LINCOLN*

## Faithful People Ask "Why"

*At seventeen, Joni Eareckson became paralyzed from the neck down because of a diving accident. Although God has not answered all her questions in the twenty-some years since, Joni continues to have faith in Him, and she inspires others to have faith as well.*

In February, 1970, my niece Kelly died of the brain tumor that had kept her in constant pain for a year. Her death underscored to me the importance of each individual soul.

I was just beginning to get a handle on a positive spiritual frame of reference myself, so Kelly's progress in faith, though she was only five, was encouraging and helpful to me as I saw the reality of God's love and power at work in her tiny life. Her tragedy brought us closer as a family and even closer to the Lord.

We had all accepted the inevitability of Kelly's death, and we had peace about it; yet this did not mean that the agony of losing her did not take its toll on us or that we did not ever ask, "Why, God?"

Kelly's mother, my sister Linda, suffered the most. Soon after Kelly became ill, Linda's husband left and divorced her. This left her with two sons and Kelly to support, along with facing Kelly's death. Her world seemed to be collapsing around her, and for a long time she didn't want to face it.

Through Kelly's death and my own paralysis, I was learning that there was nothing but unhappy frustration in trying to second-guess God's purposes. *Why God? Why did Kelly die? Why was I paralyzed? Why was someone else alive and healthy?* There was no reason apart from the overall purposes of God.

We aren't always responsible for the circumstances in which we find ourselves. However, we are responsible for the way we respond to them. We can give up in depression and suicidal despair. Or, we can look to a sovereign God who has everything under control....

God engineered circumstances. He used them to prove Himself as well as my loyalty. Not everyone had this privilege. I felt there were only a few people God cared for in such a special way that He would trust them with this kind of experience. This understanding left me relaxed and comfortable as I relied on His love, exercising newly learned trust. I saw that my injury was not a tragedy but a gift God was using to help me conform to the image of Christ, something that would mean my ultimate satisfaction, happiness—even joy.

JONI EARECKSON, *Joni* (1976)

## God Refines Our Faith

*No one likes suffering. But it brings our attention back to God and reminds us how helpless we are without Him.*

Suffering refines our faith. The trivial is excised, the essential emphasized. Do we believe God in the face of it all? If so, we will grow and be strengthened. Suffering prepares us to comfort others. Words from smiling, indifferent faces to wounded hearts mean little; but words from a fellow sufferer support and uplift. Suffering removes artificial props of security and resets the stage of our personal world with new dependence on Christ.

CHARLES STANLEY, *A TOUCH OF HIS LOVE* (1994)

*No matter what my ears may hear*
*Or what my eyes may see,*
*There's nothing for me to fear, Lord;*
*You're always here with me.*

## Faith Keeps Its Eyes on God

*David never mentions the size of the giant Goliath or how vicious he looks. What he does focus on is how faithful God has been in the past. He fully believes that God will see him through again. And He does!*

Then Saul said to David, "You are not able to go against this Philistine to fight with him; for you are but a youth while he has been a warrior from his youth."

But David said to Saul, "Your servant was tending his father's sheep. When a lion or a bear came and took a lamb from the flock, I went out after him and attacked him, and rescued it from his mouth; and when he rose up against me, I seized him by his beard and struck him and killed him.

"Your servant has killed both the lion and the bear; and this uncircumcised Philistine will be like one of them, since he has taunted the armies of the living God."

And David said, "The LORD who delivered me from the paw of the lion and from the paw of the bear, He will deliver me from the hand of this Philistine."

Thus David prevailed over the Philistine with a sling and a stone, and he struck the Philistine and killed him; but there was no sword in David's hand.

1 SAMUEL 17:33–37, 50 (NASB), *HOLY BIBLE*

## Fear Versus Faith

*We respond to stresses in our lives with either fear or faith. Fear is a great threat to our faith. That's why we read often in the Scriptures the directive, "Fear not." The closer we draw to God, the more our fears diminish.*

Jesus lived at complete liberty. The poise of his life, his absolute command of himself, his capacity to confront every exigency of his career with calm, wise, unworried, unhasting discrimination, was due to his entire independence of fear.

Not meaning, either, that he had arrived at some static position where he was forever unassailable by the various threats which life holds over every man. The general upkeep of his mood of fearlessness made certain demands. He was required to keep himself constantly in the confidence of his own source of spiritual supply. Once he was asked by a Samaritan woman where, in his opinion, was the best place to seek God.

Some said, she remarked, that God was to be sought in the holy mountain; others, the Jews, said that God was to be found in the temple at Jerusalem. Jesus told her that the time would come when men would not attempt to give God a localized address.

Jesus was not distrustful of the temple, as a fine memorial to man's reverence. He saw the point of that and commended it. He, himself, visited the temple frequently, and found it worth while. But he had to have a closer contact with God than that, to keep himself empowered with spiritual forces. He couldn't be in the temple all the time; and yet he knew he had to be conscious of God all the time. So, he conceived the practice of *living in the presence of God*.

While aware of that contact, he was beyond the reach of fear—not fears considered item by item; but *fear*. And to the maintenance of that mood, it was imperative that he keep himself free of fear-concepts. If you will go through the recorded gospels with a blue pencil and underscore all admonitions he offered on the subject of eliminating fear from human thought, you may be amazed to discover how considerable an area of his teaching was comprehended by this counsel.

And not only was he constantly urging other people to be fearless, but he was careful to avoid the contamination of their fears. He was indignant when they came howling in a panic to hurl their cowardice at him. In the storm on the Sea of Galilee, he sleeps. So confident of his own independence of physical forces was he that it was no longer necessary for him to brace himself against fear. He slept through the storm. His disciples shake him awake. What was the matter with him, anyway? Here they were, frightened to death, and he was able to sleep. Apparently they wanted him to be frightened, too. It is not enough that they be scared. He must wake up and see how serious is this menace that has stampeded them.

"Oh ye of little faith!" How often that phrase was on his lips. "Why are ye fearful . . . oh ye of little faith?"

A few days before he met his tragedy, Jesus, with his disciples, spent some time on the seacoast, near Tyre. It was a brief vacation from the wearing drain of dealing, daily, with great crowds of needy people. One day, without warning, Jesus announced that he was about to start back now, for Jerusalem. He would attend the Passover Feast. Aware of the enmities which, in Jerusalem, were being brought to a sharp focus, and would unquestionably strike at his Master on the occasion of a day of enthusiasm for the old orthodoxy, Simon Peter begged Jesus not to go. It was by no means safe. He didn't really have to go. Let him stay where he was out of the reach of his enemies. "This must not be," said Peter. Jesus pushed him aside—and not very gently, either. Peter was getting in the way—Peter with his cowardice; with his program of safety first. Jesus did not consider that an act of friendship at all. His idea of a helpful friend was someone who stimulated you to free yourself of fears; not someone who called attention to them.

Constantly, he was endeavoring to encourage other people in their faith and fearlessness.

LLOYD C. DOUGLAS, *THE LIVING FAITH* (1955)

> *"Oh ye of little faith!" How often that phrase was on his lips. "Why are ye fearful . . . oh ye of little faith?"*

## An Explorer With Faith

*It takes faith to go beyond what others know—to explore new ideas, to stand on our convictions that there is something more, and to trust that God has called us to discover it.*

He had a fine presence, a convincing way with him, due, more than anything else, to his sincere, enthusiastic belief in his own ideas. By temperament he was strongly religious. The tenets of his faith were to him living realities which never ceased to inspire his conduct, and this spiritual fervor had now extended to his belief in the mission that lay before him of discovering the lands and the peoples on the other side of the Atlantic . . .

CLIFFORD SMYTH,
*BUILDERS OF AMERICA: CHRISTOPHER COLUMBUS* (1931)

*Faith is
knowing without seeing,
believing without fully understanding,
trusting without touching
the One who is
ever faithful.*

## Promises Faithfully Kept

*Faith is more than believing in who God is. It's believing that He will keep His promises.*

Faith is not just about believing in God. It's about believing He'll do what He says—that He'll keep every promise He's made in the Holy Bible. When we are faithful, like God, we keep the promises we make. And when we have faith in another person, we believe they will keep the promises they have made.

*Faith is nurtured by love,
as the flame in a lamp is
nurtured by the oil.*

MARTIN LUTHER, *DISCOURSE ON FREE WILL*

# A Faithful Friend

*Faithful friends stick by us both when we're happy and when we're hurting—when we are nice and when we are not so nice. They put our welfare above theirs. One of life's greatest assets is a faithful friend.*

So she departed from the place where she was, and her two daughters-in-law with her; and they went on the way to return to the land of Judah.

And Naomi said to her two daughters-in-law, "Go, return each of you to her mother's house. May the LORD deal with you as you have dealt with the dead and with me.

"May the LORD grant that you may find rest, each in the house of her husband." Then she kissed them, and they lifted up their voices and wept.

And they said to her, *"No,* but we will surely return with you to your people."

But Naomi said, "Return, my daughters. Why should you go with me? Have I yet sons in my womb, that they may be your husbands?

"Return, my daughters! Go, for I am too old to have a husband. If I said I have hope, if I should even have a husband tonight and also bear sons, would you there-fore wait until they were grown? Would you therefore refrain from marrying? No, my daughters; for it is harder for me than for you, for the hands of the LORD has gone forth against me."

And they lifted up their voices and wept again; and Orpah kissed her mother-in-law, but Ruth clung to her.

Then she said, "Behold, your sister-in-law has gone back to her people and her gods; return after your sister-in-law."

But Ruth said, "Do not urge me to leave you or turn back from following you; for where you go, I will go, and where you lodge, I will lodge. Your people shall be my people, and your God, my God."

RUTH 1:7–16 (NASB), *HOLY BIBLE*

*Those of us who are strong and able in the faith need to step in and lend a hand to those who falter, and not just do what is most convenient for us.*

ROMANS 15:1 (THE MESSAGE), *HOLY BIBLE*

## Keeping the Faith

*Growing older doesn't necessitate letting go of faith. Even though our bodies are getting older and our thinking may not be as sharp as it once was, God is still the same. We can always depend on Him.*

There is another thing that we of middle life need to guard against, and that is the loss of early enthusiasms and ideals. The tendency of life's actualities is to sober and sometimes embitter. It is a difficult thing to experience trial and failure, to see the hollowness and shame, the trickery and cruelty of the social, commercial, political world, and not get cynical and skeptical—to lose, if not your faith in God, what is next worse, your faith in man and interest in man. It is hard, in contact with the actual world to preserve your faith in an ideal world, your ardor in its pursuit. The youthful vision fades, romance gives way to prosy plodding, and life's springtime grows into the hot, dusty parched summer. Oh, men and women of riper years, let us not fail to carry our earlier enthusiasms into the dry details, the grave responsibilities of later life and make the desert places rejoice and blossom as the rose!

CHARLES SUMNER HOYT, *THE OCTAVE OF LIFE* (1901)

# The Faithful Old Woman

*Having faith is believing that even small things have significance. People of faith believe that every person matters, even one person can make a difference, and that God takes small things and makes them into great things.*

An old woman who was seventy-five years old had a Sabbath-school two miles away among the mountains. One Sunday there came a terrible storm of rain, and she thought at first she would not go that day, but then she thought, "What if some one should go and not find me there?" Then she put on her waterproof, and took her umbrella and overshoes, and away she went through the storm, two miles away, to the Sabbath-school in the mountains. When she got there she found one solitary young man, and taught him the best she knew how all the afternoon. She never saw him again, and I don't know but the old woman thought her Sabbath-school had been a failure. That week the young man enlisted in the army, and in a year or two after the old woman got a letter from the soldier thanking her for going through the storm that Sunday. This young man thought that stormy day he would just go and see if the old woman was in earnest, and if she cared enough about souls to go through the rain. He found she came and taught him as carefully as if  she was teaching the whole school, and God made that the occasion of winning the young man to Christ. When he lay dying in a hospital he sent the message to the old woman that he would meet her in heaven. Was it not a glorious thing that she did not get discouraged because she had but one Sunday-school scholar? Be willing to work with one.

DWIGHT L. MOODY (1837–1899), *ANECDOTES AND ILLUSTRATIONS OF DWIGHT L. MOODY*

## People of Faith

*The Bible is filled with stories of people who had faith—people who believed what God promised and acted on those beliefs.*

By an act of faith, Abel brought a better sacrifice to God than Cain. It was what he *believed*, not what he *brought*, that made the difference. That's what God noticed and approved as righteous. After all these centuries, that belief continues to catch our notice.

By an act of faith, Enoch skipped death completely. "They looked all over and couldn't find him because God had taken him." We know on the basis of reliable testimony that before he was taken, "he pleased God." It's impossible to please God apart from faith. And why? Because anyone who wants to approach God must believe both that he exists *and* that he cares enough to respond to those who seek him.

By faith, Noah built a ship in the middle of dry land. He was warned against some-thing he couldn't see, and acted on what he was told. The result? His family was saved. His act of faith drew a sharp line between the evil of the unbelieving world and the rightness of the believing world. As a result, Noah became intimate with God.

By an act of faith, Abraham said yes to God's call to travel to an unknown place that would become his home. When he left he had no idea where he was going. By an act of faith he lived in the country promised him, lived as a stranger camping in tents. Isaac and Jacob did the same, living under the same promise. Abraham did it by keeping his eye on an unseen city with real, eternal foundations—the City designed and built by God.

By faith, barren Sarah was able to become pregnant, old woman as she was at the time, because she believed the One who made a promise would do what he said. That's how it happened that from one man's dead and shriveled loins there are now people numbering into the millions.

Each one of these people of faith died not yet having in hand what was promised, but still believing. How did they do it? They saw it way off in the distance, waved their greeting, and accepted the fact that they were transients in this world. People who live this way make it plain that they are looking for their true home. If they were homesick for the old country, they could have gone back any time they wanted. But they were after a far better country than that—*heaven* country. You can see why God is so proud of them, and has a City waiting for them.

By faith, Abraham, at the time of testing, offered Isaac back to God. Acting in faith, he was as ready to return the promised son, his only son, as he had been to receive him—and this after he had already been told, "Your descendants shall come from Isaac." Abraham figured that if God wanted to, he could raise the dead. In a sense, that's what happened when he received Isaac back, alive from off the altar.

By an act of faith, Isaac reached into the future as he blessed Jacob and Esau.

By an act of faith, Jacob on his deathbed blessed each of Joseph's sons in turn, blessing them with God's blessing, not his own—as he bowed worshipfully upon his staff.

By an act of faith, Joseph, while dying, prophesied the exodus of Israel, and made arrangements for his own burial.

By an act of faith, Moses' parents hid him away for three months after his birth. They saw the child's beauty, and they braved the king's decree.

By faith, Moses, when grown, refused the privileges of the Egyptian royal house. He chose a hard life with God's people rather than an opportunistic soft life of sin with the oppressors. He valued suffering in the Messiah's camp far greater than Egyptian wealth because he was looking ahead, anticipating the payoff. By an act of faith, he turned his heel on Egypt, indifferent to the king's blind rage. He had his eye on the One no eye can see, and kept right on going. By an act of faith, he kept the Passover Feast and sprinkled Passover blood on each house so that the destroyer of the firstborn wouldn't touch them.

By an act of faith, Israel walked through the Red Sea on dry ground. The Egyptians tried it and drowned.

By faith, the Israelites marched around the walls of Jericho for seven days, and the walls fell flat.

By an act of faith, Rahab, the Jericho harlot, welcomed the spies and escaped the destruction that came on those who refused to trust God.

HEBREWS 11:4–31 (THE MESSAGE), *HOLY BIBLE*

# God's Surprises

*When we step out and do the thing we believe God wants us to do, even if it doesn't make sense, that's faith. Our greatest rewards can come from those acts.*

Occasionally God surprises us by letting us find out how He used some word we spoke or action that we took years ago and perhaps forgot all about. About a century ago Stephen Grellat was led one day to go out to a heavily forested area of America to preach. It was a strong inward compulsion of the Holy Spirit. When he arrived at the loggers' camp, he found they had moved to another location, and their shanties were deserted. However, he was so sure he was sent by God that he went into an empty shanty and preached to the bare walls the sermon God had placed upon his heart. He then returned to his home. He could never understand why God would send him to preach to an empty shanty.

Many years later in England, as he walked across the London bridge, a man grasped his arm. "I found you at last," the man said. "I think you are mistaken," said Mr. Grellat. "No. Didn't you preach in an empty shanty in the woods of America years ago?" "Yes," Mr. Grellat admitted, "but no one was there."

"I was the foreman in charge of the loggers," the stranger explained. "We had moved to a new location before I realized I'd left one of my tools behind. I returned to get it and heard a voice in one of the shanties; I peered through a crack between the logs and saw you. You never saw me, but I listened to the rest of the sermon. God touched my heart, and I became so convicted of my sin that after some time I purchased a Bible, repented of my sins, and became a Christian. Then I began to win my men to Christ. Your sermon has led at least a thousand people to Christ, and three of them have already become missionaries!"

WESLEY L. DUEWEL, *MEASURE YOUR LIFE* (1992)

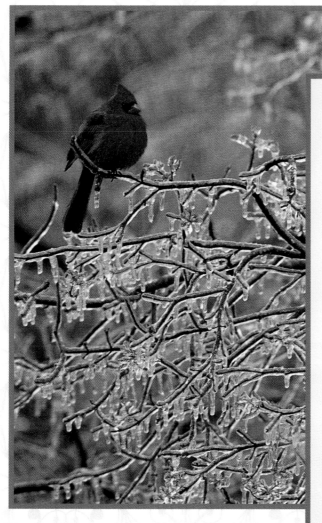

# Patience

Throughout life, one of the hardest words to hear is WAIT. Sometimes we may anxiously wonder, "Where is God when I need Him?" And yet we are reminded in Scripture, "Blessed are all those who wait for him to help them" (Isaiah 30:18, TLB). Patience is developed through faithful waiting. God has a design in even the most difficult situations that will enable our character to become stronger. As we learn patience, we also learn to trust that God has our best interests in mind. He cannot abandon us, and He will always rescue us at just the right time.

## Nature Inspires Patience

*Throughout life, patience is the virtue many people find most difficult to attain and practice. The seasonal workings of nature can provide the perfect inspiration.*

Patience. That was the virtue grandma admonished me to practice as I waited for the strawberries to ripen. It seemed the closer I watched the plants, the greener the tiny berries became! "Be patient," she said. "Them berries are on a schedule all their own, and you trampin' about in the patch won't hurry them up one bit." But patience was a hard lesson for me to learn. I wanted my marigold seeds to sprout and bloom within the week. I wanted Candy, my white-faced cow, to calf as soon as the neighbors had loaded up their bull and pulled out of our drive. But over the years, farming became a good teacher of patience. I learned that each season had its own charm as well as its own chores. I learned

to savor anticipation almost as much as realization. I tried hard to heed the advice of poet Ralph Waldo Emerson: "Adopt the pace of nature: her secret is patience."

As I grew older, I became impatient to get my driver's license, to begin dating, to graduate from high school, to enroll in college. During those adolescent years, Grandma would often open her Bible and read James 5:7–8 to me: "Be patient. . . . See how the farmer waits for the land to yield its valuable crop and how patient he is for the fall and spring rains. You too, be patient and stand firm." I would take a deep breath and promise to try.

MARY LOU CARNEY, *SPIRITUAL HARVEST* (1987)

## Teach Me to Wait Patiently

Waiting,
endless waiting.
Why does it seem impossible
to wait patiently
and
graciously—
 for the overdue phone call
 or the long-expected letter…
 for delayed company to arrive
 or a sick loved one to get better?

Is there a special ingredient
to fill the waiting time
and ease the heavy burdens
that weigh upon my mind?

Could waiting possibly achieve a work
which nothing else can do?
God, teach me how to
wait patiently
and put full trust
in You.

# The Riches of Patience

*The best way to deal with the pressures of everyday life is to patiently rely on God.*

Life is not easy to any of us. No branch escapes the pruning-knife; no jewel the wheel; no child the rod. People tyrannize over and vex us almost beyond endurance. Circumstances strain us till the chords of our hearts threaten to snap. Our nervous system is overtaxed by the run and competition of our times. Indeed, we have need of patience! . . .

And we cannot live such a life till we have learnt to avail ourselves of the riches of the indwelling Christ. The beloved Apostle speaks of being a partaker of the patience which is in Jesus (Rev. 1:9). So may we be. That calm, unmurmuring, unreviling patience, which made the Lamb of God dumb before His shearers, is ours.

F. B. MEYER, *THE SECRET OF GUIDANCE*

*Don't be impatient. Wait for the Lord, and he will come and save you! Be brave, stouthearted and courageous. Yes, wait and he will help you.*

PSALM 27:14 (TLB), *HOLY BIBLE*

*It is better to be patient than powerful; it is better to have self-control than to conquer a city.*

PROVERBS 16:32 (NLT), *HOLY BIBLE*

## Overwhelmed?

*Are insurmountable problems about to do you in? Are you nearly overwhelmed with difficulties, emergencies, and trials of all kinds?*

These may be divinely appointed instruments for the Holy Spirit to use in your life. It could take days or even weeks, but if you are patient and willing to find out how God plans to use your current struggles, they can become an avenue for spiritual growth. Problems can turn into possibilities. Tribulations can become a blessing that God could get to you in no other way. Bring all your problems to the Lord. Hold them up to Him in prayer. Sit quietly and wait for him to work. Your restless fretting accomplishes nothing. Rest! Wait! Pray! Do nothing that you are not thoroughly convinced in your spirit He is leading you to do. Give God a chance to work. The insurmountable problems that you face today will become God's opportunity to reveal His love and grace to you as you have never known before.

## Patience Develops Character

We can rejoice, too, when we run into problems and trials for we know that they are good for us—they help us learn to be patient. And patience develops strength of character in us and helps us trust God more each time we use it until finally our hope and faith are strong and steady.

ROMANS 5:3–4 (TLB), *HOLY BIBLE*

## Learning to Live Patiently

Rejoice when I run into problems?
Know trials are good for me?
Things like that aren't easy—
Learning to live patiently.

Growing in grace is a process.
Developing character hurts.
Becoming more Christ-like in all things
Is an everyday process called work.

But if I have faith it is possible.
Faith knowing God loves and cares—
That all my burdens and trials
He also feels and shares.

## Use Your Trials

*The trials that come into our lives are the opportunities through which we learn patience.*

Use your trials. What is the purpose of the testing? God makes our trials the instrument of blessing. Too often our trials work impatience, but God will give grace that His real purpose may be accomplished. Patience is more necessary than anything else in our faith life. We forget that time is nothing with God, for with Him a thousand years is as one day, and one day as a thousand years. Christ's purpose in our lives is that we shall be perfect and entire, wanting nothing.

HENRIETTA C. MEARS, *WHAT THE BIBLE IS ALL ABOUT* (1953)

## The Patience of Faith

*We may need to endure hard times, but we can trust that whatever happens is part of God's plan.*

Patience is more than endurance. A saint's life is in the hands of God like a bow and arrow in the hands of an archer. God is aiming at something the saint cannot see, and He stretches and strains, and every now and again the saint says—"I cannot stand any more." God does not heed, He goes on stretching till His purpose is in sight, then He lets fly. Trust yourself in God's hands. For what have you need of patience just now? Maintain your relationship to Jesus Christ by the patience of faith. "Though He slay me, yet will I wait for Him."

OSWALD CHAMBERS, *MY UTMOST FOR HIS HIGHEST* (1935)

## Patience I Don't Easily Learn

God, I know you're not in a hurry —
Your plans for me are on time.
You need no schedule or reminders
For I'm always on your mind.

I know you have drawn the mosaic
And You're fitting each tile in place.
As I continue to follow your plan,
Help me not to hurry or race.

Waiting is so often difficult,
And patience I don't easily learn.
But to have my life more Christ-like
Is for what I seek and yearn.

So as my life's pattern continues
And the next part begins to unfold,
It's you I'm trusting and praising,
It's your hand I cling to and hold.

## I Must Be Patient

*"On the day I called, you answered me, you increased my strength of soul" (Psalm 138:3, NRSV).*

God hears my cries for help, and
He answers every prayer.
I only need be patient—
He supplies the "how" and "where."

Sometimes it may be immediate
In a tangible way I'll know;
While other times I wait assured
That He is strengthening my soul.

His grace is all-sufficient
To meet my heart-cries need.
As I lean upon His promises,
Walking in faith, He'll lead.

*A patient man has great understanding,
but a quick-tempered man displays folly.*

PROVERBS 14:29 (NIV), *HOLY BIBLE*

## Learning to Wait Patiently

*We often need to patiently endure time and experience in order to be fully prepared for whatever it is God has planned for our lives. This is illustrated in the Bible by the wilderness experience of Moses, who spent eighty years in preparation for the commission God gave him.*

It had taken years, but now Moses had slowed down enough from the maddening pace of life to have time to stop and listen.

"I will go over and see this strange sight—why the bush does not burn up," he mused.

From that moment, all his life was altered. The door, which had been closed so long it resembled the wall, suddenly opened. For as he approached the bush, a voice spoke, calling him by name: "Moses, Moses!"

That voice still speaks to wilderness wanderers. Though the day may seem to be a day like every other

day, and the bush like all bushes, things are not always as they seem. Elizabeth Barrett Browning captured the concept:

Earth's crammed with heaven,
And every common bush afire with God;
But only he who sees takes off his
     shoes. . . .

The tragedy of our wilderness experience is not that we have to go through grief and suffering, but that we often miss the blessings from burning bushes—the things through which God speaks. Through a letter from a friend, the words of a book, a long-forgotten song, the voice of a teacher, the beauty of a holy life, the innocence of a child, God still calls us by name and makes His eternal purpose known. . . .

Learning to wait patiently, learning to do today what your hand finds to do, learning to hear the call of God when it comes, and to respond—that is what the wilderness is all about. Once a man submits his life to God's control, he voluntarily surrenders the right to determine or the power to vary the consequences of that decision. From that moment on, no situation can ever come into the life of the believer which has not first passed through the hands of God and thus had redeeming quality. . . .

To all those wandering in the wilderness, let it be said: bushes still catch on fire and God still calls men by their names. But the call comes only to those who are busy with the smaller tasks already assigned.

JAMIE BUCKINGHAM, *A Way Through the Wilderness* (1986)

## To Be Patient

*The process of growing up is lifelong. Maturity is reflected when we respond calmly and wisely to problems.*

The capacity to be patient and to refrain from judgment, the willingness to listen and to be able to control our emergent feelings—the fact the we stop for a moment—these are signals that we live at an adult level.

EUGENE KENNEDY, *The Trouble With Being Human* (1986)

*Be glad for all God is planning for you. Be patient in trouble, and always be prayerful.*

ROMANS 12:12 (NLT), *HOLY BIBLE*

## Pray With Patience

*"And we know that all things work together for good to them that love God, to them who are called according to His purpose" (Romans 8:28, KJV).*

Should you, however, not at once obtain answers to your prayers, be not discouraged; but continue patiently, believingly, perseveringly to wait upon God: and as assuredly as that which you ask would be for your real good, and therefore for the honor of the Lord; and as assuredly as you ask it solely on the ground of the worthiness of the Lord Jesus, so assuredly you will at last obtain the blessing. I myself have had to wait upon God concerning certain matters for years, before I obtained answers to my prayers; but at last they came.

GEORGE MULLER

*But they that wait on the Lord shall renew their strength; they shall mount up with wings as eagles; they shall run, and not be weary; and they shall walk, and not faint.*

ISAIAH 40:31 (KJV), *HOLY BIBLE*

*If you've tried and have not won,
Never stop for crying;
All that's great and good is done
Just by patient trying.*

PHOEBE CARY (1824–1871)

## Forty Days and Nights

*One of the all-time favorite Bible stories is that of the Great Flood. Besides being a wonderful story, it also provides valuable lessons about patience and faith.*

I can see Noah and his three sons felling the huge cypress trees, hacking off the bark and hewing the trunks into water-worthy planks, while their wicked peers jeered and shouted insults. For years they worked on that boat, in a spot so far inland that a scarcity of water seemed a more impending threat than a profusion of rain. As he hammered and planed and sawed, Noah preached. His topic was always the same: repentance. But his neighbors were more interested in sensual pleasures, in greed and gluttony, in idolatry and innocent bloodshed.

Then the rains began. Drops the size of grapes plopped onto the dust around the ark. Their patter turned to pounding, and inside the ark Noah and his family knew it was true. God was destroying the world. Only they and the animals on board would survive.

For the next year, Noah and the others on the ark lived in a world of bobbing isolation. At first they heard the cries of now-penitent people, the terrified screams of jackals and wolves. But soon these sounds were silenced by the slosh of waves, by the reality of water rising higher than the mountains.

> *"He waited. He did not pace in panic. He waited."*

What patience Noah had! During those long years of labor, during those long months of confinement, he did not rant or rail. He waited. He did not pace in panic. He waited. And one morning, as sunlight streamed through the solitary window and patterned the worn deck, Noah knew it was time. He released a dove. She came back by nightfall, unable to find a resting place. For almost a month he sent forth this bird. Although he longed for respite from his watery world—longed to see the rough beauty of tree bark and to feel the earth beneath his feet—Noah knew that this was no time to be impulsive. It was no time to lead the remnants of creation into an unsure situation. Finally, the dove did not return. Then Noah was certain that the ground was indeed dry, that the fury of God's judgment had passed.

The huge door of the ark creaked open. Foxes and camels blinked into the brightness. Birds fluttered their folded wings and fumbled into flight. Lions tossed their manes as memories stirred of star-filled nights spent stalking prey.

What did Noah do? Rush headlong out into this new world? Boast at having beaten the odds? Organize committees to establish a new community? Hardly! "Then Noah built an altar to the Lord and, taking some of all the clean animals and clean birds, he sacrificed burnt offerings on it" (Genesis 8:20). Even in this time of great jubilation, of enormous challenge, Noah's priorities and patience were intact. He paused to offer thanks. And God, pleased with Noah, promised never again to destroy all living creatures.

> "As long as the earth endures,
> seedtime and harvest,
> cold and heat,
> summer and winter,
> day and night
> will never cease."
> Genesis 8:22

What did Noah do then? He planted a vineyard, and, sure of God's promise, settled down to watch it grow. To *patiently* watch it grow.

MARY LOU CARNEY, *SPIRITUAL HARVEST* (1987)

*Maturity: facing each new day with patience, calmness, and confidence that God is in control.*

## Let Patience Have Her Perfect Work

*Any great work of art takes time to be perfected in the hands of the master artist.*

Let patience have her perfect work. Statue under the chisel of the sculptor, stand steady to the blows of his mallet. Clay on the wheel, let the fingers of the divine potter model you at their will. Obey the Father's lightest word: hear the Brother who knows you and died for you.

GEORGE MACDONALD, *RIGHTEOUSNESS*

*Brothers and sisters, we urge you to warn those who are lazy. Encourage those who are timid. Take tender care of those who are weak. Be patient with everyone.*

1 THESSALONIANS 5:15 (NLT), *HOLY BIBLE*

# Honesty

We all prefer to deal with honest people — people we can trust — people who will not lie or try to deceive us. A noble goal for one's life is to pursue honesty — honesty with others, with ourselves, and with God. Yet it is not natural to tell the truth. Honesty can seem to leave us open to attack — to tear down the walls of protection we would rather erect in our lives. Scripture tells us, "The truth shall make you free." Although it might be hard to be honest, if we do it with loving intentions, the burden that dishonesty brings will be lifted.

## The Depths of Honesty

*Honesty is more than just not telling lies. It begins inside us with our motives and moves outward to how we deal with people.*

Honesty is more complex than simply not stealing money or not telling a bold lie. Honesty involves our deepest motives and encompasses every area of private and public life. It includes truth in every sense, and integrity in the inner person. Honesty demands putting aside lying, cheating, slander, and deceit—and, at times, even silence.

JERRY WHITE, *HONESTY, MORALITY & CONSCIENCE* (1979)

## Qualities of an Honest Man

*What we do when a lie is exposed determines our level of honesty. An honest person sincerely desires to face up to their lies and get back to the truth.*

An honest man is not a man who never lies. There is no such man. When an honest man is caught in a lie or discovers he has lied, he is quick to admit it. He then speaks the truth. He's not afraid to say, "Please forgive me for not being honest." He does not defend a lie. Unlike a dishonest man, he does not make plans to lie or use lies to cover other falsehoods. He regularly scrutinizes his life to see if he has lied or is living a lie in any area. Honesty with God, his fellow man, and himself is the honest man's goal and his heart's desire.

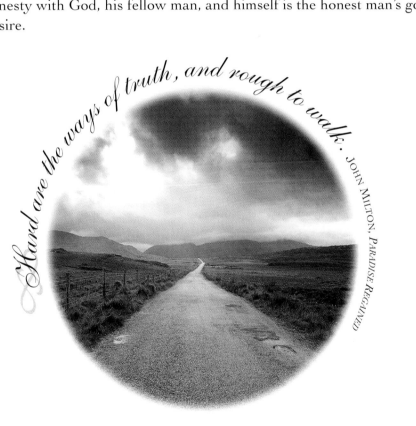

*Hard are the ways of truth, and rough to walk.* JOHN MILTON, *PARADISE REGAINED*

# The High Cost of Dishonesty

*It's sometimes hard to face others with the truth and deal with the consequences. But if we keep the truth concealed, we will always pay the price.*

Loisel possessed eighteen thousand francs which his father had left him. He borrowed the rest. . . .

When Mrs. Loisel took back the jewels to Mrs. Forestier, the latter said to her in a frigid tone:

"You should have returned them sooner, for I might have needed them."

She did open the jewel-box as her friend feared she would. If she should perceive substitution, what would she think? What would she say? Would she take her for a robber?

Mrs. Loisel now knew the horrible life of necessity. She did her part, however, completely, heroically. It was necessary to pay this frightful debt. She would pay it. They sent away the maid; they changed their lodgings; they rented some rooms under a mansard roof.

She learned the heavy cares of a household, the odious work of a kitchen. She washed the dishes, using her rosy nails upon the greasy pots and the bottoms of the stewpans. She washed the soiled linen, the chemises and dishcloths, which she hung on the line to dry; she took down the refuse to the street each morning and brought up the water, stopping at each landing to breathe. And, clothed like a woman of the people, she went to the grocer's, the butcher's, and the fruiterer's, with her basket on her arm, shopping, haggling, defending to the last sou her miserable money.

Every month it was necessary to renew some notes, thus obtaining time, and to pay others.

The husband worked evenings, putting the books of some merchants in order, and nights he often did copying at five sous a page.

And this lasted for ten years.

At the end of ten years, they had restored all, all, with interest of the usurer, and accumulated interest besides.

Mrs. Loisel seemed old now. She had become a strong, hard woman of the poor household. Her hair badly dressed, her skirts awry, her hands red, she spoke in a loud tone, and washed the floors, using large pails of water. But sometimes, when her husband was at the office, she would seat herself before the window and think of that evening party of former times, of that ball where she was so beautiful and so flattered.

> *"How small a thing will ruin or save one!"*

How would it have been if she had not lost that necklace? Who knows? Who knows? How singular is life, and how full of changes! How small a thing will ruin or save one!

One Sunday, as she was taking a walk in the Champs-Elysees to rid herself of the cares of the week, she suddenly perceived a woman walking with a child. It was Mrs. Forestier, still young, still pretty, still attractive. Mrs. Loisel was affected. Should she speak to her? Yes, certainly. And now that she had paid, she would tell her all. Why not?

She approached her. "Good morning, Jeanne."

Her friend did not recognize her and was astonished to be so familiarly addressed by this common personage. She stammered:

"But, Madame—I do not know—You must be mistaken—"

"No, I am Matilda Loisel."

Her friend uttered a cry of astonishment: "Oh! my poor Matilda! How you have changed—"

"Yes, I have had some hard days since I saw you; and some misterable ones—and all because of you—"

"Because of me? How is that?"

"You recall the diamond necklace that you loaned me to wear to the Commissioner's ball?"

"Yes, very well."

"Well, I lost it."

"How is that, since you returned it to me?"

"I returned another to you exactly like it. And it has taken us ten years to pay for it. You can understand that it was not easy for us who have nothing. But it is finished and I am decently content."

Madame Forestier stopped short. She said:

"You say that you bought a diamond necklace to replace mine?"

"Yes. You did not perceive it then? They were just alike?"

And she smiled with a proud simple joy. Madame Forestier was touched and took both her hands as she replied:

"Oh! my poor Matilda! Mine were false. They were not worth over five hundred francs!"

GUY DE MAUPASSANT, FROM "THE DIAMOND NECKLACE," IN *SELECTED TALES OF GUY DE MAUPASSANT*

## God's View of Lies

*Honesty is obviously a very important trait in God's eyes. He detests lying so much that it is mentioned twice on this list of things he hates.*

There are six things the LORD hates, seven that
are detestable to him:
haughty eyes,
a lying tongue,
hands that shed innocent blood,
a heart that devises wicked schemes,
feet that are quick to rush into evil,
a false witness who pours out lies
and a man who stirs up dissension among brothers.

PROVERBS 6:16–19 (NIV), *HOLY BIBLE*

*No legacy is so rich as honesty.*

WILLIAM SHAKESPEARE (1564–1616),
*ALL'S WELL THAT ENDS WELL*

*Dishonesty builds a wall between two people. Only the hammer of truth can break the wall down.*

## Dishonesty Under Pressure

*We are all capable of dishonesty. Even Jesus' close friend Peter lied when he was under pressure and his life seemed in danger. Later, though, he traveled around boldly proclaiming the truth.*

The soldiers lit a fire in the courtyard and sat around it for warmth, and Peter joined them there.

A servant girl noticed him in the firelight and began staring at him. Finally she spoke: "This man was with Jesus!"

Peter denied it. "Woman," he said, "I don't even know the man!"

After a while someone else looked at him and said, "You must be one of them!"

"No sir, I am not!" Peter replied.

About an hour later someone else flatly stated, "I know this fellow is one of Jesus' disciples, for both are from Galilee."

But Peter said, "Man, I don't know what you are talking about." And as he said the words, a rooster crowed.

At that moment Jesus turned and looked at Peter. Then Peter remembered what he had said—"Before the rooster crows tomorrow morning, you will deny me three times." And Peter walked out of the courtyard, crying bitterly.

LUKE 22:55–62 (TLB), *HOLY BIBLE*

## Honesty Versus Keeping the Peace

*Being honest with our feelings is difficult, but dishonesty builds walls in relationships. When we are honest with others about how we feel, we are drawn closer together.*

Years ago I saw a television show where a camera was hidden in a restaurant. An actor entered, sat next to a man eating at the counter, and without saying a word, grabbed some French fries off the man's plate. This scenario was repeated numerous times, and nine times out of ten the victims never said a word. You knew they were doing a slow burn inside; they clenched their fists and glared at the thief in disbelief. But they never said a word.

When people submerge their true feelings in order to preserve harmony, they undermine the integrity of a relationship. They buy peace on the surface, but underneath there are hurt feelings, troubling questions, and hidden hostilities just waiting to erupt. It's a costly price to pay for a cheap peace, and it inevitably leads to inauthentic relationships.

BILL HYBELS, *HONEST TO GOD?* (1990)

## Part of Love Is Honesty

*It's not always easy to tell the truth when another person asks us a question. Many times we know they don't really want to hear the truth. Yet, if we want love to grow, honesty is a fertile soil.*

If I really love you, don't I have to be honest with you? When you ask me, "Was it me? Or was it them?" when caught in a conflict, I can't always take your side, even though it seems like the loving thing to do. But is it really loving, or just easiest? If I truly love you, I will stop being afraid to say, "My friend, sometimes you are wrong." I don't want to listen to the lie anymore—the one that says, "If you love and accept me, you will never confront me." I want what's best for you, and sometimes that best will

come when I am honest about the worst I see in you. The test of true love comes when I speak the truth in love—when I risk being honest about your dark side. If you walk away, then I know that although I loved you enough to be honest, you did not love me enough to let me be.

## Telling the Truth About Pain

*Sometimes we put up a false front, even with our closest friends and loved ones. We think, "What would happen if they knew what's really going on with me?" When we stop hiding behind a "happy face," we open the door to true intimacy.*

Too often we lie
when people say,
How are you?
We say, "I'm fine."
We smile, and put
on our happy face.

Why can't we be honest,
at least with loved ones,
and say, "I hurt"?
Why can't we cry honest tears
and let a friend
comfort us for a moment —
embrace us
with loving arms,
as we take off
the mask we wear
to hide the pain?

*Lying lips are an abomination to the LORD, But those who deal truthfully are His delight.*

PROVERBS 12:22 (NKJV), *HOLY BIBLE*

## Telling Ourselves the Truth

*Though we may feel noble when we brutally tell people the truth about their faults, we need to be honest about our own faults first. After we've done that, our honesty becomes gentler.*

"Do not judge lest you be judged yourselves.

"For in the way you judge, you will be judged; and by your standard of measure, it shall be measured to you.

"And why do you look at the speck in your brother's eye, but do not notice the log that is in your own eye?

"Or how can you say to your brother, 'Let me take the speck out of your eye,' and behold, the log is in your own eye?

"You hypocrite, first take the log out of your own eye, and then you will see clearly enough to take the speck out of your brother's eye."

MATTHEW 7:1–5 (NASB), *HOLY BIBLE*

# Plunging Into the Depths of Honesty

*The truth can be difficult to face, but if we are always desiring to seek and face the truth, our lives will be much richer. Being willing to dig deeper for truth is a sign of godliness.*

Our work is not only to be done thoroughly, but it is to be done honestly. A man is not only to be honorable in his academic relations, but he must be honest with himself and in his attitude toward the truth. Students are not entitled to dodge difficulties, they must go down to the foundation principles. Perhaps the truths which are dear to us go down even deeper than we think, and we will get more out of them if we dig down for the nuggets than we will if we only pick up those that are on the surface. Other theories may perhaps be found to have false bases; if so, we ought to know it. It is well to take our soundings in every direction to see if there is deep water; if there are shoals we ought to find out where they are. Therefore, when we come to difficulties, let us not jump lightly over them, but let us be honest as seekers after truth.

HENRY DRUMMOND,
*THE GREATEST THING IN THE WORLD* (1891)

# Truth and Consequences

Be brave, my soul—
Let go of lies.
Stop deceiving yourself.
Have courage
to embrace the truth
and all its consequences.

*An honest man's the
noblest work of God.*

ALEXANDER POPE, "AN ESSAY ON MAN"

## Move On to Telling the Truth

Don't lie to one another. You're done with that old life. It's like a filthy set of ill-fitting clothes you've stripped off and put in the fire. Now you're dressed in a new wardrobe.

COLOSSIANS 3:9–10 (THE MESSAGE),
*HOLY BIBLE*

*Honesty is the best policy.*

MIGUEL DE CERVANTES (1547–1616), *DON QUIXOTE*

## Honesty as a Student

*Many people defend lying, because "everyone is doing it." To go along with the lies of others is to be dishonest ourselves. It takes courage to expose dishonesty.*

The chatter in the room dwindled to a few nervous comments and jokes as the professor began passing out the exams. Several students hastily reviewed their notes. Others sat nervously tapping their pencils on the desks. The normal pre-exam tension filled the air, accompanied by sweaty palms and jittery stomachs.

The professor gave a few brief words of explanation and walked out of the room, leaving two student proctors to monitor the exam and answer questions. There was a rustle of relief as soon as he left. Crib sheets emerged, books opened, and dozens of students began cheating blatantly.

One student, however, saw the obvious cheating and became inwardly agitated. A former cadet at the United States Air Force Academy, he was now working on a special assignment to complete his master's degree. He had been trained for four years under an honor code at the academy.

Finally, he stood up and announced to the class, "What you people are doing is wrong! It is cheating! I can't stand for it and I plan to report this to the instructor!"

He sat down as abruptly as he had stood. The class was speechless. Then a new wave of nervousness swept across the room.

After the exam several students congratulated the student for his courage. Cheating bothered them too, they said, but it was so common they had felt unable to do anything.

The student reported the cheating, and the exams were discarded and a new test was administered. What was accomplished by his action? It didn't stop all the cheating, but a clear standard of right was established in the class. Others were given courage to act on their convictions in the future, and the student himself had a strengthened sense of integrity and the peace of a clear conscience.

JERRY WHITE, *HONESTY, MORALITY & CONSCIENCE* (1979)

## Solomon's Wisdom About Honesty

Lies will get any man into trouble, but honesty is its own defense (Proverbs 12:13, TLB).

Telling the truth gives a man great satisfaction ... (Proverbs 12:14, TLB).

A good man is known by his truthfulness; a false man by deceit and lies (Proverbs 12:17, TLB).

Truth stands the test of time; lies are soon exposed (Proverbs 12:19, TLB).

## Honorable Title

I hope I shall always possess firmness and virtue enough to maintain what I consider the most enviable of all titles, the character of an "Honest Man."

GEORGE WASHINGTON, IN A LETTER TO
ALEXANDER HAMILTON, AUGUST 28, 1788

## We Need God's Help to Be Honest

We can never be completely honest on our own.
It is human nature to lie.
That's why when a witness
who takes the stand in a court of law is asked,
"Do you solemnly swear
to tell the truth, the whole truth,
and nothing but the truth,"
the phrase is added,
"so help me God."

## Honesty Means We Stop Pretending

*Honest people are real, especially before God.*
*When we pretend that everything is fine or that*
*we are self-sufficient, the one that ends up*
*getting hurt is us. Pretending only weakens us*
*and our relationships.*

If we could stop pretending to be strong
and start being honest with ourselves and God,
crying out, "God, please help!
I am poor and needy,"
He would hurry to help us
and be the strength of our lives.

*. . . and you will know*
*the truth, and the truth will*
*set you free.*

JOHN 8:31 (TLB), *HOLY BIBLE*

# Forgiveness

*Forgiveness is the central virtue in God's treasure chest—God's forgiveness of us, and our forgiveness of others, God, and ourselves. We've all stood in the midst of the Sunday congregation praying, "Forgive us our sins as we forgive those who sin against us." At times we find that forgiveness comes very easily, even for grievous and painful hurts. But many times, we seem powerless to forgive, no matter how hard we try. This is when God's forgiving grace has the opportunity to touch and change us and then be extended to others through our example.*

## Forgiveness

Snow
that fell
so softly in the night
changed earth's soot to white
in glistening loveliness.

Forgiveness
like soft snow
gently covers the soil
and lo
ugliness is beauty!

LUCILLE GARDNER

## Preparing to Forgive

*Our emotional release of the past and its pain will, in a large measure, determine our ability to move on into constructive future relationships.*

Forgiveness is letting what was, be gone; what will be, come; what is now, be.

In forgiving, I finish my demands on past predicaments, problems, failures and say good-by to them with finality. I cancel my predictions, suspicions, premonitions of failure and welcome the next moment with openness to discover what will be. I make a new transaction of affirming integrity between us now....

Forgiveness is willingly accepting the other on the basis of our loving and leveling, of our caring and confronting, agreeing to be genuine with each other here, now and in the future.

Forgiveness is being willing to let it be with the best that we can achieve now and move on into the future without repressing my own spontaneous response to you or seeking to restrict yours.

DAVID AUGSBURGER, *CARING ENOUGH TO FORGIVE* (1981)

# The Biblical Theme of Forgiveness

*Because none of us will ever be able to live a perfect life, we need to be understanding and practice forgiveness in our daily lives.*

Forgiveness is a theme that runs throughout the pages of the Bible. When we confess our sins to Jesus Christ, we are promised that he will forgive (1 John 1:9). Then, in the Lord's prayer, we are instructed to forgive others just as Christ forgave us (Matthew 6:12).

To forgive is to pardon completely and to forget the offense forever, without holding a grudge and without maintaining an attitude of condescending superiority because of what we have done.

There are times when every human being loses control. We explode in anger, say things that should not have been said, gossip, harbor jealousy or envy...or otherwise give in to subtle temptations. Sometimes we admit these tendencies, at least to ourselves, and recognize the presence of guilt because of our thoughts or actions. At other times we pretend to "have it all together" and walk about like the Pharisees of old claiming to be something that we are not....

Whenever we lose control or slip into sin we can confess directly to God and know for certain that he will forgive without requiring that we do anything to atone for our wrongdoing.

At times, however, there can be value in confessing not only to God but to our fellow human beings. One way to care for others is to confess to one another, pray for one another, forgive one another, and accept each other with all of our human imperfections (James 5:16; Ephesians 4:32; Romans 15:7). Since God is clearly willing to forgive, we have a responsibility to do the same.

GARY R. COLLINS, *THE JOY OF CARING* (1980)

# Ask Forgiveness, Pick Yourself Up, and Try Again

*God prefers that we make an effort, even if we should initially fail. He will eagerly forgive our mistakes in the hope that we will learn and grow from them.*

We may, indeed, be sure that perfect chastity—like perfect charity—will not be attained by any merely human efforts. You must ask for God's help. Even when you have done so, it may seem to you for a long time that no help, or less help than you need, is being given. Never mind. After each failure, ask forgiveness, pick yourself up, and try again. Very often what God first helps us towards is not the virtue itself but just this power of always trying again. For however important chastity (or courage, or truthfulness, or any other virtue) may be, this process trains us in habits of the soul which are more important still. It cures our illusions about ourselves and teaches us to depend on God. We learn, on the one hand, that we cannot trust ourselves even in our best moments, and, on the other, that we need not despair even in our worst, for our failures are forgiven. The only fatal thing is to sit down content with anything less than perfection.

C. S. LEWIS, *MERE CHRISTIANITY* (1943)

Forgive us, Lord, our sins, for failing to live
up to your standards of goodness and justice.
We confess our shortcomings. Make us
willing to change and help us become persons
of godly character. Amen.

## Redemption

*God knows that as hard as we may try, there are
times when we will make human mistakes. Even
so, if we trust in Him and ask His forgiveness,
He will bless us with mercy and peace.*

The Lord hath spoken peace to my soul,
He hath blessed me abundantly,
Hath pardoned my sins;
He hath shown me great mercy and saved me
     by his love.
I will sing of his goodness and mercy while
     I live,
And ever, forever will praise his holy name.
O how sweet to trust in God,
And to know your sins forgiven,
To believe his precious word,
And be guided by his love.
Therefore goodness and mercy,
Shall follow me all the days of my life.
Amen.

C. E. LESLIE, *LESLIE'S CROWN OF SONG* (1890)

## Mercy, Forgiveness, and Pardon

*These three words, as taught from an 1896 school textbook, appear to be similar on the surface, yet they are very different when we look closely at the definitions.*

*Mercy* is the exercise of less severity than one deserves, or in a more extended sense, the granting of *kindness* or *favor* beyond what one may rightly claim. *Grace* is *favor, kindness,* or *blessing* shown to the undeserving; *forgiveness, mercy* and *pardon* are exercised toward the ill-deserving. *Pardon* remits the outward penalty which the offender deserves; *forgiveness* dismisses resentment or displeasure from the heart of the one offended; *mercy* seeks the highest possible good of the offender. . . .

To *pardon* is to let pass, as a fault or sin, without resentment, blame, or punishment. *Forgive* has reference to feelings, *pardon* to consequences; hence, the executive may *pardon*, but has nothing to do officially with *forgiving.* Personal injury may be *forgiven* by the person wronged; thus, God at once *forgives* and *pardons*; the *pardoned* sinner is exempt from punishment; the *forgiven* sinner is restored to the divine favor. To *pardon* is the act of a superior, implying the right to punish; to *forgive* is the privilege of the humblest person who has been wronged or offended.

JAMES C. FERNALD, *ENGLISH SYNONYMS AND ANTONYMS* (1896)

## Feelings or Fact?

*The story is told that someone asked Martin Luther (1483-1546) if he "felt" that he had been forgiven. His reply:*

> "No, but I'm as sure
> As there's a God in Heaven.
> For feelings come, and feelings go,
> And feelings are deceiving.
> My warrant is the Word of God,
> Naught else is worth believing."

And thus it has remained with all men down through the ages. Many times we may come to the place where it is difficult to "feel" forgiven. That is where faith comes in. And the very basis of the Christian faith is a belief in a God that cannot lie. "I acknowledged my sin unto thee, and mine iniquity have I not hid. I said, I will confess my transgressions unto the Lord; and thou forgavest the iniquity of my sin" (Psalm 32:5, KJV).

*Forgiveness is the soil in which God nurtures our emotional healing and our ability to love once again.*

JOHN NIEDER AND THOMAS M. THOMPSON,
*FORGIVE & LOVE AGAIN* (1991)

## Jesus Teaches Forgiveness

*This familiar Bible story clearly illustrates that when we are shown mercy, we must pass that gift on to others.*

It was Peter who came to Jesus with another question.

"Lord," he said, "how often should I forgive my brother? If he keeps sinning against me, should I forgive him seven times?"

Jesus said, "I do not say seven times, but seventy times seven. Peter, my rock, this is the way that it is in the kingdom of heaven—." Then Jesus told this parable.

"Once upon a time," he said, "a king decreed that everyone who owed him money should pay it at once. But one of his servants owed him ten thousand talents, an enormous sum, an impossible debt.

"'Pay me!' said the king.

"'O sir!' said the servant, 'I cannot pay you.'

"The king frowned. 'Very well,' he said, 'then I shall have to sell you and your wife and your children into slavery!'

"When the servant heard that, he began to cry. He sank to his knees and folded his hands and wailed, 'Wait! Wait! I will work for it, sir! Have patience with me, and I will work and pay every penny I owe.'

"'Let me see,' said the king, and he fell to figuring. He added, and he multiplied, and he discovered that it would take this servant one hundred and fifty thousand years to pay back the debt if he worked for it.

"That made the king feel very sorry for his servant. 'No,' he said, 'do not try to work that long. Instead, I forgive you the whole debt.' He struck a line through his account books and said, 'You owe me nothing any more. Go in peace.'

"That servant bowed very often, being very happy, and left the palace.

"But as soon as he was outside, he saw another servant who owed *him* a hundred denarii. He grabbed the poor man by the throat and said, 'Pay me!'

"'O sir!' said the fellow servant, 'I cannot pay you.'

"'Ha!' he said. 'And I suppose you expect me to wait while you work for it?'

"'Have patience, sir, and I will pay you,' said the fellow servant.

"'Patience?' he said. 'I have figured it out. You would have to work a hundred days in order to pay me back. No, I cannot have that much patience!' And he had his fellow servant thrown into prison.

"When the king heard what his servant had done, he stood up and roared, 'Get him!'

"'You wicked servant!' said the king. 'I forgave you your debt because you asked me. Why could you not have mercy on your fellow servant, even as I had mercy on you? *Take this man away!*'

"The king gave the servant to the jailers. The jailers put him in prison. And there he sat until the whole ten thousand talents should be paid.

"Even so," said Jesus, "will my Heavenly Father do to you if you do not forgive your brother from your heart."

MATTHEW 18:21–35, AS TOLD BY WALTER WANGERIN, JR., IN *THE BOOK OF GOD FOR CHILDREN* (1981)

# Beware of Witholding Forgiveness

*When we receive God's forgiveness, we should pass it freely on to others. Our example is Christ, who was willing to forgive even those who crucified him.*

Our sins are forgiven by God's mercy alone. We can't earn forgiveness by forgiving others. But when we withhold forgiveness from others after having received it ourselves, it shows we don't understand or appreciate God's mercy toward us.

JAMES 2:13 (TLB), *LIFE APPLICATION BIBLE NOTES*

You will be judged on whether or not you are doing what Christ wants you to. So watch what you do and what you think; for there will be no mercy to those who have shown no mercy. But if you have been merciful, then God's mercy toward you will win out over his judgment against you.

JAMES 2:12–13 (TLB), *HOLY BIBLE*

## Psalm 32

Blessed is he whose transgression is forgiven, whose sin is covered. Blessed is the man unto whom the LORD imputeth not iniquity, and in whose spirit there is no guile.

When I kept silence, my bones waxed old through my roaring all the day long.

For day and night thy hand was heavy upon me: my moisture is turned into the drought of summer. Selah.

I acknowledged my sin unto thee, and mine iniquity have I not hid. I said, I will confess my transgressions unto the LORD; and thou forgavest the iniquity of my sin. Selah.

For this shall every one that is godly pray unto thee in a time when thou mayest be found: surely in the floods of great waters they shall not come nigh unto him.

Thou art my hiding place; thou shalt preserve me from trouble; thou shalt compass me about with songs of deliverance. Selah.

I will instruct thee and teach thee in the way which thou shalt go: I will guide thee with mine eye.

Be ye not as the horse, or as the mule, which have no understanding: whose mouth must be held in with bit and bridle, lest they come near unto thee.

Many sorrows shall be to the wicked: but he that trusteth in the LORD, mercy shall compass him about.

Be glad in the LORD, and rejoice, ye righteous: and shout for joy, all ye that are upright in heart.

*The Holy Bible* (KJV)

## The Experience of Finding Forgiveness

*To live life having been forgiven means that we endeavor, with God's help, to walk in obedience on the pathway He has chosen for us.*

God is committed to forgiving sin so thoroughly that He will put it out of His mind, out of remembrance, and out of sight. This is a great truth to grasp.

Often I have found myself in a position where I have been required to forgive someone, but the thoughts that I harbor concerning that person reveal that my forgiving has certainly not included forgetting. But real forgiveness forgets. . . .

The experience of finding forgiveness is not without its pressures. The psalmist explains something of the battle that went on in his life as he became increasingly conscious of his sin and more aware of the necessity for dealing with it. David was under considerable pressure from the Lord, which he describes in such graphic

phrases as "my bones waxed old through my roaring" / "Thy hand was heavy upon me" / "my moisture is turned into the drought of summer" (Psalm 32:3–4).

In other words, David was suffering from such guilt and conviction that he was dry and depressed and thoroughly upset. The longer he "kept silence," the worse it became, but when he came to the point of "acknowledging and confessing," he was able to say, "Thou forgavest my sin" (v. 5).

Beware of the mistaken idea that once confession has been made and forgiveness received, we, as Christians, are free to go on as before. Be perfectly clear in your mind that being forgiven does not leave you free to go on in the same way. Rather, it introduces you to a new responsibility to be different. . . .

The ongoing of the forgiven life is dependence on the Lord to instruct and a response to the Lord in obedience. The Lord then undertakes to lead in the right path.

STUART BRISCOE, *WHAT WORKS WHEN LIFE DOESN'T* (1976)

# Forgiveness — The Precondition of Love

*Forgiveness is not dependent on our feelings, but is rather a determination of our will.*

Forgiveness is the precondition of love. The "how" of forgiveness is through knowing how to use our will—the rudder of our life. We are responsible for the set of this rudder; once we have willed a course of action, God will be responsible for our feelings if we will hand them over to Him. Otherwise, nothing we can do would change these feelings.

When I put that conclusion along side David du Plessis' statement, "Forgiveness means, 'The other person may be as wrong as wrong can be, but I'll not be the judge,'" I saw that forgiveness is simply the decision of our wills to release a particular person, followed by verbalizing that to God. It can be a simple prayer like, "Lord, I release _____ from my judgment. Forgive me that I may have bound him and hampered Your work by judging. Now I step out of the way so that Heaven can go into action for _____." Obviously, there is nothing impossible about praying like that.

CATHERINE MARSHALL, *SOMETHING MORE* (1974)

*A few well-chosen words of forgiveness are like an antiseptic that cleanses the wound and promotes healing.*

## Divine Forgiveness

*The biblical story of the prodigal son reminds us that God is eager to forgive us, and it prompts us to be ready to forgive others.*

To understand divine forgiveness we must turn to the teachings of Jesus. His parable of the prodigal son illustrates it best. The younger of two sons leaves home in reckless, youthful disregard of the father's love. In a distant country he squanders his money with dissolute companions who desert him when his money is gone. Reduced to tending swine—unspeakable depths to a Jew—he begins to compare his hunger and loneliness with the abundance and love he had experienced at home. Suddenly he resolves to return home: "I will arise and go to my father, and I will say to him, 'Father I have sinned...'" (Luke 15:11–24).

The father rushes down the road to welcome the returning son. The young man begins his carefully rehearsed speech of repentance, but the father cuts it short with his glad welcome. The son's repentance is obvious; nothing matters to the father but that his son has returned. The father has not waited until now to extend forgiveness. In his mind the son was always forgiven. But he could not be aware of or accept or be healed by that forgiveness until he returned in repentance.

CECIL OSBORNE, *THE ART OF UNDERSTANDING YOURSELF* (1967)

# An Unlikely Forgiveness

*For decades, preachers have retold this story of the late Rev. Mr. Lee, who was a Presbyterian minister in Waterford, New York. He serves as a good example of a man with a forgiving spirit.*

It was midnight. Mr. Lee was still in his study preparing the Sunday morning sermon. Suddenly a strange noise aroused him. He felt the presence of someone else in the room.

"Who is it? What is the matter?" he called, turning around in his desk chair.

He was face-to-face with a grim burglar pointing a gun directly at him. The robber, thinking that all of the occupants were fast asleep, had entered the house through a side window.

"Give me your watch and money," he demanded, "and make no noise or I will shoot."

"You may put down your gun. I will make no resistance. You are at liberty to take all of the valuables I possess," was Mr. Lee's calm reply. "I will lead you to where my most precious treasures are stored."

They walked down the hall where he opened the door to an adjoining room. He pointed to the bed where his two children lay innocently sleeping. "Those," he said, "are my choicest jewels. Will you take them?"

He proceeded to tell the would-be burglar that, as a minister of the Gospel, he owned very few earthly possessions. What little money he did earn was all devoted to one purpose—to educate these two motherless children.

The burglar was deeply and visibly moved by these remarks. Tears filled his eyes as he said, "Please, sir, forgive me, I didn't know. I am so sorry to have troubled you, and so sorry for the act which I was about to commit."

Mr. Lee's well-chosen words convicted this would-be criminal. Then he invited him to kneel right there and join him in prayer.

God had softened the heart of this burglar and he consented to pray the sinner's prayer, pouring forth his remorse and penitence.

Mr. Lee was able to assure him of the Scripture, "If we confess our sins, he is faithful and just to forgive us our sins, and to cleanse us from all unrighteousness" (1 John 1:9, KJV). Mr. Lee showed the man to the door with these words, "Go, and sin no more."

*Now is the time to forgive this man and help him back on his feet. If all you do is pour on the guilt, you could very well drown him in it. My counsel now is to pour on the love.*

2 CORINTHIANS 2:7 (THE MESSAGE), *HOLY BIBLE*

## A Healing Prayer

*Only by calling on God for help are we able to truly forgive and forget.*

Father, we praise you for your healing mercy. Thank you for loving and accepting us with all our hurts, hangups and sins, but thank you even more for caring enough to change us. Thank you for saving us from ourselves and our unwittingly self-destructive tendencies. We reach out and open up to receive your tender mercies, praising you for showing us that we are forgiven so that we may be able to forgive—both ourselves and others! Amen.

JON EARGLE, *HEALING WHERE YOU HURT ON THE INSIDE* (1981)

## The Practice of Forgiveness

*Even if we feel we've been wronged by someone, if we soften our hearts and forgive the one who wronged us, the burden of bitterness will be lifted. This change is certain to affect the lives of those around us.*

There is nothing more healing in all the world than when one starts to practice forgiveness. It's not always easy to forgive, but it's far more difficult not to. When Jesus was so unjustly treated, how did he react? The answer is he didn't react, he responded. Jesus—the responder—forgave them. Jesus cried as the blood spurted from his heart, "Father, forgive them, for they know not what they do." Jesus taught that we were to forgive an unlimited number of times (Matthew 18:21, 22). Disciples asked the Lord how many times they should forgive and Jesus said seven times seventy. Then he added that if we don't forgive others, then we can't be forgiven our sins.

*Only the offended can forgive.*

A wife was left alone evening after evening. Her resentments turned to hate. She started keeping a hate book, actually writing down in a notebook every night her husband was gone from home, and the exact number of minutes. It got so bad he spent only two evenings home in seven weeks, always finding excuses to be away. His wife would constantly badger him about this in the few minutes he would be home.

Then the lady began to respond to God's working in her heart. He showed her what her bitter unforgiving spirit was doing, how in the few minutes her husband was at home, she was driving him further and further away from home and herself. She read the challenge of Christ in her Bible, to be the first to forgive. Her life took a turn for the better when she said with God's help, "I forgive him." Then she had a second great thought. If she was going to forgive him, it meant throwing the hate book away. She took the hate book and threw it in the fire. That was followed by a great idea. The idea was this—"I will make the most out of those moments when he is home, and make it interesting and pleasant."

Within weeks he began spending more time at home and soon afterward he faced up to the way he had been shortchanging his family. Foundations were laid for a new and more satisfying relationship in the home. Forgiveness is what brought the breath of fresh air and newness to this home.

*Forgiveness has healed many a broken relationship, and forgiveness has healed many a wounded spirit.*

The healing medicine—forgiveness—is yours for the using.

DALE E. GALLOWAY, *DREAM A NEW DREAM* (1975)

## Perfect Forgiveness

*Sometimes it may seem impossible to forgive other people, especially if they are purposely trying to hurt us. But if Jesus could forgive the people who crucified Him, certainly we can forgive those who have hurt us.*

When on the fragrant sandal-tree
    The woodman's axe descends,
And she who bloomed so beauteously
    Beneath the keen stroke bends,
E'en on the edge that wrought her death
Dying she breathed her sweetest breath,
As if to token, in her fall,
Peace to her foes, and love to all.

How hardly man this lesson learns,
To smile and bless the hand that spurns;
To see the blow, to feel the pain,
But render only love again!
This spirit not to earth is given—
One had it, but he came from heaven.
Reviled, rejected, and betrayed,
No curse he breathed, no plaint he made,
But when in death's deep pain he sighed
Prayed for his murderers, and died.

AUTHOR UNKNOWN

*Judge not, and ye shall not be judged: condemn not, and ye shall not be condemned: forgive, and ye shall be forgiven . . .*

LUKE 6:37 (KJV), *HOLY BIBLE*

## How to Destroy Your Enemies

An elderly woman asked Abe Lincoln, "How can you speak kindly of your enemies when you should rather destroy them?"

"Madam," he said, "do I not destroy them when I make them my friends?"

CARL SANDBURG

## Forgive and You'll Be Forgiven

For if you forgive people their trespasses — that is, their reckless and willful sins, leaving them, letting them go and giving up resentment — your heavenly Father will also forgive you.

But if you do not forgive others . . . neither will your Father forgive you your trespasses.

MATTHEW 6:14–15 (AMPLIFIED), *HOLY BIBLE*

# Forsaking Revenge

*Too many times we dwell on the wrongs that have been done against us, and we determine that it is impossible for us to forgive another. The following is a paraphrase of a story told in Tolstoy's* Russian Stories and Legends *(Pantheon Books).*

An honest and hardworking Russian peasant named Aksenov left his dear wife and family for a few days to visit a nearby fair. He spent his first overnight at an inn during which a murder was committed. The murderer placed the murder weapon in the sleeping peasant's bag. The police discovered him that way in the morning. He was stuck in prison for twenty-six years, surviving on bitter hopes of revenge. One day the real murderer was imprisoned with him and soon charged with an escape attempt. He had been digging a tunnel that Aksenov alone had witnessed. The authorities interrogated the peasant about his crime granting him at long last his opportunity for revenge, for on the peasant's word his enemy would be flogged almost to death.

Aksenov was asked to bear witness to the crime, but instead of jumping at the chance, the grace of God suddenly wells up in the peasant's heart, and he finds the darkness in him has fled, and he is filled with light. He finds himself saying to the officers: "I saw nothing."

That night the guilty criminal makes his way to the peasant's bunk and, sobbing on his knees, begs his forgiveness. And again the light of Christ floods the peasant's heart. "God will forgive you," said he. "Maybe I am a hundred times worse than you." And at these words his heart grew light and the longing for home left him.

CHARLES R. SWINDOLL, *THE QUEST FOR CHARACTER* (1987)

## Love Depends on Forgiveness

*Love and forgiveness walk hand-in-hand. Our relationships with God and others are intertwined in this dynamic.*

Love often succumbs to a cold death on the sharp rocks of disappointment. *Love cannot last long or live out its eternal purpose in human relationships without a foundation of forgiveness* — the forgiveness from God for our failure to love with a pure, other-centered heart, and forgiveness when the recipient of our love spurns our gift or uses our soul in an unloving fashion. Unless the fabric of our involvement with others is woven with the threads of forgiveness, love will suffer the corruption of denial, hardness, cynicism, and eventually hatred....

Love is dependent on forgiveness. A formula can almost be structured from this concept. *The extent to which someone truly loves will be positively correlated to the degree the person is stunned and silenced by the wonder that his huge debt has been canceled.* Perhaps another way to say it is that gratitude for forgiveness is the foundation for other-centered love.

Dr. Dan B. Allender, *Bold Love* (1992)

## What Is Forgiveness?

*Whatever the relationship, forgiveness is
a truly healing gift for the people involved.
In a marriage, the power of true forgiveness
cannot be overstated.*

Forgiveness is, at the same time, a pure, supernatural giving: the receiver doesn't deserve it; the giver wants nothing for it. It's not a *thanks*giving, because that's the return of one goodness for another. It's not a purchasing price, not even the price of marital peace, because that is hoping to buy one goodness with another. Forgiveness is not a good work which expects some reward in the end, because that motive focuses upon the giver, while this kind of giving must focus completely upon the spouse, the one receiving the gift, the one who sinned. The forgiver cannot say, "Because I have given something to you, now you must give something to me." That's no gift at all.

Rather, forgiveness is giving love when there is no reason to love and no guarantee that love will be returned. The spouse is simply not lovable right now! Forgiveness is repaying evil with kindness, doing all the things that love requires—even when you don't *feel* the love; for you can *do* love also in the desert days when you do not feel loving.

Only when a pure, unexpected, unreasonable, and undeserved gift-giving appears in the marriage does newness enter in and healing begin. This is grace. Only when the spouse has heard his sin, so that he might anticipate, under the law, some retribution, but receives instead the gestures of love—only then can he begin to change and grow in the same humility which his wife has shown him. Finally, gift-giving is the greatest sacrifice of all, for it is the complete "giving away" of one's self.

WALTER WANGERIN, JR., *As for Me and My House* (1987)

## Steps of Forgiveness

*First we are hurt, and feelings of anger may consume us. Then thoughts of how we can get revenge come creeping in. But only when we are ready to relinquish the hurt is there an opportunity for forgiveness and healing to begin.*

Forgiveness demands we get in touch with our anger, bitterness—and get past the denial of built-up resentments. We cannot be bitter and be led by God at the same time. Unconsciously we may say, "I choose to react toward them with bitterness." We choose our attitude in any circumstance. Unfortunately, we seldom vent our anger at the person to whom it is intended, but rather family members and friends must bear the brunt of our outbursts.

Forgiveness is not always possible on our own. That's when we must pray, "God, in my own strength it is impossible for me to forgive. I am ready to be made willing to forgive this person. Help me find the strength to make the phone call or write the letter that will begin the healing process."

Total forgiveness means first we ask God for forgiveness of our poor attitude and seek his help (1 John 1:9). Then we must go to the other party and ask their forgiveness (James 5:16). And as we ask, we must be ready and willing to offer forgiveness (Matthew 6:14–15).

Forgiveness is a mark of a virtuous life. "Do not repay anyone evil for evil. Be careful to do what is right in the eyes of everybody. If it is possible, as far as it depends on you, live at peace with everyone. Do not take revenge, my friends, but leave room for God's wrath, for it is written: 'It is mine to avenge; I will repay,' says the Lord" (Romans 12:17–19, NIV).

It is only as we thank God for His forgiveness that we sense our anger and bitterness slipping away and are able to get on with the process of living.

## Forgiveness Leads to Reconciliation

*Forgiveness can be a critical issue among family members—especially around the holiday season.*

Suppose all those people who are dreading the holidays could forgive the individuals who wounded them and those who have perpetrated the hurts would be willing to apologize and ask for forgiveness? Wouldn't that remove the spectre-like overtones which often obscure the joy of the holidays?

It may seem to be an overly simplistic solution, but the Scriptures clearly teach that forgiveness is essential to reconciliation and restoration of broken relationships.

Of course, it is not in our power to cause another person to apologize and seek forgiveness from us. But conducting our own personal "attitude check-up" is something each of us can and should do. We should be as diligent about getting rid of unforgiveness in our hearts as a cardiologist would be about dealing with plaque in our arteries. One is as great a threat to our spiritual health as the other is to our physical health.

How tragic to hear of a young man being stricken in the prime of life with deadly heart disease, often a treatable condition he was unaware of. Even more tragic is a person of any age who has allowed unforgiveness to corrode his soul and poison his spirit, while defending his right to bear a grudge. That kind of corrosion kills one's spiritual life and also affects one's physical well-being.

RUTHANNE GARLOCK, *HOW TO FORGIVE YOUR CHILDREN* (1989)

*I will forgive their iniquity, and I will remember their sin no more.* JEREMIAH 31:34B (KJV), *HOLY BIBLE*

An apology is a friendship preserver, an antidote for hatred, never a sign of weakness; it costs nothing but one's pride, always saves more than it costs, and is a device needed in every home.

AUTHOR UNKNOWN

Praise the Lord, I tell myself, and never forget the good things he does for me. He forgives all my sins and heals all my diseases. He ransoms me from death and surrounds me with love and tender mercies.

PSALM 103:2–4 (NLT), *HOLY BIBLE*

136

## The High Cost of Getting Even

*When we are shamefully wronged by someone and can't resist the temptation to get even, the effects may be felt in the diseases of our body and mind.*

For centuries scoffers have ridiculed the advice of Jesus, "Love your enemies," as being impractical, idealistic and absurd. Now psychiatrists are recommending it as a panacea for many of man's ills.

When Jesus said, "Forgive seventy-times seven," He was thinking not only of our souls, but of saving our bodies from ulcerative colitis, toxic goiters, high blood pressure, and scores of other diseases. The advice of the Great Physician appears to have percolated even into the hard-boiled bulletin of a Milwaukee police department: "If selfish people try to take advantage of you, cross them off your list, but don't try to get even. When you try to get even, you hurt yourself more than you hurt the other fellow."

Booker T. Washington, who became famous in spite of prejudice against his color, and who was insulted times without number, wrote, "I will not let any man reduce my soul to the level of hatred."

The famous physiologist, John Hunter, knew what anger could do to his heart: "The first scoundrel that gets me angry will kill me." Some time later at a medical meeting, a speaker made assertions that incensed Hunter. As he stood up and bitterly attacked the speaker, his anger caused such a contraction of the blood vessels in his heart that he fell dead....

Paul, who was convicted as he witnessed the stoning of Stephen and heard his prayer, outlines the steps toward getting rid of the disease-producing spirit of retaliation:

So put to death those members that are on earth.... Once you moved among them, when you lived in them; but off with them all now, off with anger, rage, malice, slander....you have stripped off the old nature with its practices, and put on the new nature.... be clothed with compassion, kindliness, humility, gentleness, and good temper—forbear and forgive each other in any case of complaint; as Christ forgave you, so must you forgive. And above all you must be loving, for love is the link of the perfect life (Colossians 3:5, 7–10, 13–14, Moffatt).

S. I. McMillen, M.D., *None of These Diseases*

## The Forgiving Life

*It takes both the grace of God and an act of our will to purposely forget when we've been wronged.*

Develop the fine art of forgetting petty wrongs and unkind acts. "Be kind to one another, tenderhearted, forgiving each other," Paul urged the Christians at Ephesus (4:32, NASB). A friend of Clara Barton, founder of the American Red Cross, once reminded Clara of an especially cruel thing done to her years before. "Don't you remember it?" her friend asked. "No," came the reply, "but I do distinctly remember forgetting it."

No one can be free and happy by harboring grudges. "Seek peace and pursue it" is good advice. Long before modern psychology determined that unresolved anger has the potential of making one physically ill, the Bible offered healthy words: "See to it...that no root of bitterness springing up causes trouble" (Hebrews 12:15, NASB).

EDWARD I. HAYES, *THE FOCUSED LIFE* (1985)

# Generosity

We all have numerous resources from which to share. Having a "generous spirit" does not mean simply giving money. Time is another precious commodity, and generous volunteers enable many organizations to function well: hospitals, schools, missions, animal shelters, community centers, nursing homes, child-care centers, churches—and the list goes on. Look around. What do you have to share? A "spirit of generosity" means openhandedly giving time, energy, and creativity, as well as monetary resources. Great is the reward of the person who generously gives whatever he or she has to help others.

*A generous man will prosper; he who refreshes others will himself be refreshed.*

PROVERBS 11:25 (NIV), *HOLY BIBLE*

## Prove Your Faith With Generosity

*True faith is demonstrated when we look for ways to be kind and generous to those in need.*

Dear brothers and sisters, what's the use of saying you have faith if you don't prove it by your actions? That kind of faith can't save anyone. Suppose you see a brother or sister who needs food or clothing, and you say, "Well, good-bye and God bless you; stay warm and eat well"—but then you don't give that person any food or clothing. What good does that do?

So you see, it isn't enough just to have faith. Faith that doesn't show itself by good deeds is no faith at all—it is dead and useless.

JAMES 2:15–17 (NLT), *HOLY BIBLE*

## God Loves a Cheerful Giver

Remember this: Whoever sows sparingly will also reap sparingly, and whoever sows generously will also reap generously. Each man should give what he has decided in his heart to give, not reluctantly or under compulsion, for God loves a cheerful giver.

2 CORINTHIANS 9:6–7 (NIV), *HOLY BIBLE*

*One man gives freely, yet grows all the richer; another withholds what he should give, and only suffers want.*

PROVERBS 11:24 (RSV), *HOLY BIBLE*

## A Poor Widow Gives All She Has

*This story from the Holy Bible lets us know that giving a small amount graciously is much more important than giving a large amount grudgingly.*

Then he went over to the collection boxes in the Temple and sat and watched as the crowds dropped in their money. Some who were rich put in large amounts. Then a poor widow came and dropped in two pennies. He called his disciples to him and remarked, "That poor widow has given more than all those rich men put together! For they gave a little of their extra fat, while she gave up her last penny" (Mark 12:41–44, TLB).

In the Lord's eyes, this poor widow gave more than all the others put together, although her gift was by far the smallest. The value of a gift is not determined by its amount, but by the spirit in which it is given. A gift given grudgingly or for recognition loses its value. When you give, take heart—small gifts are more pleasing to God than large gifts when they are given out of gratitude.

*LIFE APPLICATION BIBLE NOTES*

*It is more blessed
to give than to receive.*

ACTS 20:25 (KJV), *HOLY BIBLE*

## The Reward of Generous People

All goes well for those who are
generous, who lend freely and conduct
their business fairly. Such people will
not be overcome by evil circumstances.
Those who are righteous will be long
remembered. They do not fear bad
news; they confidently trust the Lord
to care for them. They are confident
and fearless and can face their foes
triumphantly. They give generously
to those in need. Their good deeds
will never be forgotten. They will
have influence and honor.

PSALM 112:5–9 (NLT), *HOLY BIBLE*

## God's Generous Character

*In Scripture, God's laws reflect His generous character.*

When you harvest your crops, do not harvest the grain along the edges of your fields, and do not pick up what the harvesters drop. It is the same with your grape crop—do not strip every last bunch of grapes from the vines, and do not pick up the grapes that fall to the ground. Leave them for the poor and the foreigners who live among you, for I, the Lord, am your God.

LEVITICUS 19:9–10 (NLT), *HOLY BIBLE*

But if someone who is supposed to be a Christian has money enough to live well, and sees a brother in need, and won't help him—how can God's love be with him?

1 JOHN 3:17 (TLB), *HOLY BIBLE*

I want you to share your food with the hungry and to welcome poor wanderers into your homes. Give clothes to those who need them, and do not hide from relatives who need your help.

ISAIAH 58:7 (NLT), *HOLY BIBLE*

## Giving to the Poor

Charity—giving to the poor—is an essential part of Christian morality.... I do not believe one can settle how much we ought to give. I am afraid the only safe rule is to give more than we can spare. In other words, if our expenditure on comforts, luxuries, amusements, etc., is up to the standard common among those with the same income as our own, we are probably giving away too little. If our charities do not at all pinch or hamper us, I should say they are too small. There ought to be things we should like to do and cannot do because our charitable expenditure excludes them.

C. S. LEWIS, *MERE CHRISTIANITY*

## Do What You Can

*This little poem was written for the Lend-a-Hand Society. It serves as a good reminder that each of us can make a difference in our own way.*

I am only one,
But still I am one.
I cannot do everything,
But still I can do something;
And because I cannot do everything
I will not refuse to do the something that
I can do.

EDWARD EVERETT HALE (1822–1909)

*We are mature individuals not when we know what we want and how to get it but when we understand what we possess of value and know how to give it away freely.*

EUGENE KENNEDY, *THE TROUBLE WITH BEING HUMAN* (1986)

## Too Great a Gift to Keep

*Some gifts are simply too special to keep to ourselves. The great storyteller Bob Benson tells this story of an African man who shared his greatest gift with others.*

I once heard a missionary tell a very moving story about an African man to whom he had given a copy of the Bible. The African was so grateful for that gift, and so profuse in his thanks, that the missionary was puzzled a few months later when they met again. For the Bible was battered and torn and it looked as though many of the pages were missing.

"I thought you would have taken better care of the Bible I gave you," he remarked. "I assumed you wanted it and would treasure it."

And the African man replied, "It is the finest gift I ever received. It is such a wonderful book that I gave a page to my father and a page to my mother and then I gave a page to everyone in the village."

BOB BENSON, *SEE YOU AT THE HOUSE* (1986)

# Be Always Giving

*All earthly creatures have a responsibility to give. Plants,*
*animals, even bodies of water, all work together to create a*
*balanced environment. We, too, must do our fair share.*

The sun gives ever; so the earth—
What it can give so much 'tis worth;
The ocean gives in many ways—
Gives baths, gives fishes, rivers, bays;
So, too, the air, it gives us breath
When it stops giving, comes in death.
> Give, give, be always giving;
> Who gives not is not living;
> > The more you give
> > The more you live.

God's love hath in us wealth unheaped
Only by giving it is reaped;
The body withers, and the mind
Is pent up by a selfish rind.
Give strength, give thought, give deeds, give pelf
Give love, give tears, and give thyself.
> Give, give, be always giving,
> Who gives not is not living;
> > The more we give
> > The more we live.

AUTHOR UNKNOWN

# He Gave His All

*God compels us all to give of ourselves in different ways. For some people that may even mean giving the ultimate sacrifice of life.*

Dr. Paul Carlson, the martyred medical servant of the people of Congo, was a college classmate and friend of mine. We had studied together, traveled together and in general kept in contact with each other for some time before he went to Africa.

Answering the call of the United Nations to furnish desperately needed medical help at the time of Congo's independence and revolution, Paul dedicated himself to do the obviously loving thing. He went to Africa because he was prepared to alleviate the existing need. A godly compulsion to give all of himself characterized his life.

After a couple of years, Paul's work, and that of a medical student assistant, caught the attention of a leading magazine, and a major news feature and picture story was prepared for publication. But as he was assisting the suffering, the great uprising occurred. He was captured by Congolese rebels, the Simbas, who claimed he was a foreign agent. While he was held prisoner in Stanleyville, thousands of us prayed impatiently for his release. After all, the rebels were not known for humanitarian behavior. When he and other prisoners were not released, rescue operations began. Planes were sent in an attempt to return as many captives as possible to safety. When the planes landed, the prisoners broke for freedom. But Paul's life ended in a hail of machine-gun bullets.

Immediately the story and pictures of his work, and the message of the supreme love of God for man that motivated him, was flashed throughout the world. Of his life one television commentator said, "Paul asked only for the opportunity to give, and it cost him his life."

The motivation and inspiration of his work were not lost, however. Today a medical foundation in the Congo continues Paul's selfless giving.

LLOYD H. AHLEM, *DO I HAVE TO BE ME?* (1973)

*Every man shall give as he is able, according to the blessing of the Lord thy God which He hath given thee.*

DEUTERONOMY 16:17 (KJV), *HOLY BIBLE*

*When you help the poor you are lending to the Lord—and he pays wonderful interest on your loan!*

PROVERBS 19:17 (TLB), *HOLY BIBLE*

## Becoming a Generous Giver

*To become truly generous in spirit, we must change the way we think about our possessions.*

When we say, "Please enter—my house is your house, my joy is your joy, my sadness is your sadness and my life is your life," we have nothing to defend, since we have nothing to lose but all to give. Turning the other cheek means showing our enemies that they can only be our enemies while supposing that we are anxiously clinging to our private property, whatever it is: our knowledge, our good name, our land, our money, or the many objects we have collected around us. But who will be our robber when everything he wants to steal from us becomes our gift to him? Who can lie to us, when only the truth will serve him well? Who wants to sneak into our back door, when our front door is wide open?

HENRI J. M. NOUWEN, *REACHING OUT* (1975)

What can I give Him,
Poor as I am?
If I were a shepherd
I would bring a lamb,
If I were a Wise Man
I would do my part,
Yet what can I give Him,
Give my heart.

CHRISTINA GEORGINA ROSSETTI (1830–1894)

God gave because
He is love. It was the
best He had to offer.
The supreme gift.
The total gift. In the
person of His Son,
He gave Himself.

Instead of a gem or a flower, cast the gift of a lovely thought into the heart of a friend. GEORGE MacDONALD (1824-1905)

The compassionate person builds up his own reservoir of peace, confidence, creativity, excitement, and resourcefulness and then generously shares it all as an encourager of others.

## Give What You Have

Be it health or be it leisure,
Be it skill we have to give,
Still in spending it for others
Christians only really live.

Not in having or receiving,
But in giving, there is bliss;
He who has no other pleasure
Ever may rejoice in this.

AUTHOR UNKNOWN

*All our opportunities, abilities, and resources come from God. They are given to us to hold in sacred trust for Him. Cooperating with God will permit us to generously pass on to others some of the many blessings from His rich storehouse.*

# Integrity

When we think of integrity, we think of someone who is honorable and trustworthy—a person who keeps their word and guards their reputation. To be called a man or woman of integrity is a high compliment. Such a person knows the difference between right and wrong and diligently pursues doing right, no matter what the obstacles. Jesus provides the best example of a man of integrity; He was not swayed by outer influences but lived a life above reproach. Integrity comes not just from the pursuit of right living, but the pursuit of God, which leads to right living.

# Integrity:
# The Ultimate Virtue

*Do we prize integrity above the tangible things in life? Are we concerned with being what we say we are? To become a person of integrity is a high calling and one worth pursuing.*

The dictionary uses words such as *whole* and *complete* to describe what integrity means. *To borrow a modern expression, a man with integrity "has his act together."* There are no loose ends that threaten his reputation.

Recently I ran across a full-page ad for an international relief organization. The picture shows a young child—perhaps from Central America or possibly Asia—writing at her desk. The ad copy contains the following sentence: "Integrity. It's as simple as being what you say you are." That strikes me as an excellent definition of integrity. It means being what you say you are—*all* the time and in *every* situation.

To be called a man of integrity is the highest possible compliment. Several years ago my older brother took me to visit a cemetery outside Florence, Alabama, near the remains of an antebellum mansion called Forks of Cypress. The mansion was built in the 1820s by James Jackson, an early settler of northwest Alabama. My brother and I walked among the ruins of the mansion and then crossed the country road into the dense forest on the other side. After a quarter of a mile we found the Jackson family cemetery. There is no sign marking the spot, only a five-foot-high stone wall surrounding about fifty graves. Inside we found a tall marker over James Jackson's grave, with a long inscription extolling his virtues, which were many.

As I walked along, my eyes fastened on the marker for one of his sons, William Moore Jackson. There was his name, the dates 1824–1891, and this simple five-word epitaph: "A man of unquestioned integrity."

Five words to sum up an entire life. Sixty-plus years distilled into five words. But, oh, what truth they tell.

"A man of unquestioned integrity." I cannot think of a better tribute. Then the thought came: "What will they put on my tombstone?"

I'm not sure what anyone will write on my tombstone. But I wouldn't mind if someone felt I deserved those five words.

RAY PRITCHARD, *THE ABC'S OF WISDOM* (1997)

## Integrity Defined

*A person of integrity is concerned not just with doing right but with right motives and right thinking.*

Integrity is a wholesome or moral completeness, and is characteristic of a person whose life reflects the life of Jesus Christ. Integrity demonstrates the inner person—the motive behind the act.... Integrity encompasses all of what we do and are—speech, motives, and actions. A mature Christian walks in integrity, inwardly and outwardly.

JERRY WHITE, *HONESTY, MORALITY & CONSCIENCE* (1979)

## Integrity and Responsibility

*Many view saying, "I was wrong," or "I need help," as signs*
*of weakness. Only when we are willing to say these things*
*are we taking steps toward true strength.*

Integrity and responsibility go together.
People of integrity take responsibility
    rather than blaming others for their wrong behavior.
A person of integrity is not afraid to say,
    "I was wrong," and "Will you forgive me?"
    He or she has the courage to say, "I need help.
    I can't make it alone."
People of integrity
    are not afraid to tell others of their weaknesses,
and they discover ways to conquer them.

# A Call to Integrity

*People of integrity keep the promises they make. They are true to their word whether in business, their family lives, or in their relationship with God.*

We have a unique opportunity today, the chance to stand up, be counted, and give men who have chosen a different road an alternative before it's too late. We need to recapture the spiritual climate in our own homes and cultivate a heart for other men. Our homes, men, are about to collapse. The homes we live in are coming apart at the seams. But we can't just worry about our own homes. We've got to foster regard and concern for the homes around us. Together we must stand up and be counted for Almighty God.

To accomplish all this, to till the rough ground of this hostile culture and plant some new seeds for Christ, each of us must commit to model what I call the three non-negotiables of manhood: integrity, commitment and action.

If you were to take the word integrity and reduce it to its simplest terms you'd conclude that a man of integrity is a promise-keeper. He's a guy who, when he says something, can be trusted. When he gives his word, you can take it to the bank. His word is good.

BILL McCARTNEY, FORMER FOOTBALL COACH AND FOUNDER OF PROMISE KEEPERS, *WHAT MAKES A MAN?* (1992)

## Integrity in Youth

*Parents teach children integrity by what they do, not what they say. Organizations like the Girl Scouts and Boy Scouts attempt to instill integrity in children, so they will grow up honorably.*

### The Girl Scout Law

I will do my best to be
    honest and fair,
    friendly and helpful,
    considerate and caring,
    courageous and strong, and
    responsible for what I say and do,
and to
    respect myself and others,
    respect authority,
    use resources wisely,
    make the world a better place, and
    be a sister to every Girl Scout.

*JUNIOR GIRL SCOUT HANDBOOK*

## On My Honor

*Our honor is our good name, our public esteem, our reputation. God desires that we act honorably, desiring to do the right thing even if no one sees us—even if others refuse to do right.*

### The Girl Scout Promise

On my honor, I will try:
    To serve God and my country,
    To help people at all times,
    And to live by the Girl Scout Law.

*JUNIOR GIRL SCOUT HANDBOOK*

# Learning Integrity

*When we see people of integrity, one comment we can make about them is that they have grown up. They no longer react to life in the ways they did as a child. They have allowed God to raise them above that.*

Few men know how to live. We grow up at random carrying into mature life the merely animal methods and motives which we had as little children. And it does not occur to us that all this must be changed, that much of it must be reversed; that life is the finest of Fine Arts; that it has to be learned with lifelong patience, and that the years of our pilgrimage are all too short to master it triumphantly.

Yet this is what Christianity is for — to teach men THE ART OF LIFE.

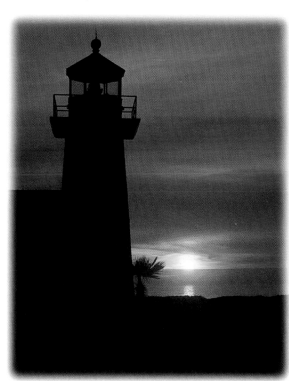

And its whole curriculum lies in one word — "Learn of me." Unlike most education, this is almost purely personal; it is not to be had from books, or lectures or creeds or doctrines. It is a study from the life. Christ never said much in mere words about the Christian graces. He lived them, He was them. Yet we do not merely copy Him. We learn His art by living with Him, like the old apprentices with their masters.

HENRY DRUMMOND,
*THE GREATEST THING IN THE WORLD* (1891)

## People Notice a Person of Integrity

*When a person of integrity is in a position of leadership, people may notice something "different" about them. This provides an opportunity for them to point to God as the source of their integrity.*

When asked if he thought a year ago, when the team was languishing in its usual misery, if this turnaround was possible, he said he relied on his religious faith.

This would sound hokey out of any-body's mouth but Tony Dungy's. He isn't a football coach. He's a gentleman. In a game driven only by money and muscle, in a sport that has warped the culture, he is so different that he can strike you as weird.

On Monday, he didn't hype himself. He didn't jump up and down. He talked about how nice it was to be stopped at the mall by well-wishers.

I say this with some discomfort, as one of those people who raised their voices against giving Dungy's boss the store, and a new stadium, too.

All those columns contained one question: Wasn't anything else more important than keeping a football team for a community with so many great and crying needs?

The answer was, and is, yes. Schools, parks, law and order, we recite the litany instantly.

That rare commodity, values, is also on the list.

You can't buy them.

But you can get Tony Dungy. The man embodies the best ones. He's focused. He's soft-spoken. He's steady. The first thing you see when you meet him is not an ego the size of Montana. The next thing you think is that every school child should meet him. And his wife. And his family.

It's easy, of course, to say this now that he's made the Bucs rise from the dead. So easy the words sound cheap.

But football's values are so screwy, he got points taken off during the commentators' reviews for not going bonkers on the sidelines Sunday night. Football's values are so screwy that, if the Bucs blow what they've begun, critics will say Tony Dungy isn't man enough for the job. Isn't mean and violent enough.

Football's values are our values, and our values also made a very qualified man wait longer than he should have to become a coach, because he came in the wrong color.

Tony Dungy's values are different. The miracle may continue, or the Bucs may go down in flames. Either way, we'll be watching a man of character at work.

MARY JO MELONE, FROM "TORNADO OF BUCS
HYPE SWIRLS PAST A QUIET PILLAR," *ST. PETERSBURG TIMES*,
SEPTEMBER 23, 1997, AFTER THE TAMPA BAY BUCANEERS
WON THEIR FIRST FOUR GAMES

*How far that little candle throws his beams! So shines a good deed in a naughty world.*

WILLIAM SHAKESPEARE (1564–1616),
*THE MERCHANT OF VENICE*

## Refusing to Compromise

*When we make a decision to do right, there will most likely be opposition. It is a test of a person's integrity to stand firm during those trying times, as is evident from the true story below.*

Eric said simply but with great firmness, "I'm afraid there are no ways, sir." The others stared at him. "I cannot run on the Sabbath and that's final...."

"Don't be impertinent, Liddell," snapped Lord Adogan.

"The impertinence lies, sir, with those who seek to influence a man to deny his beliefs. God made countries and God makes kings and the rules by which they govern," said Eric. "Those rules say the Sabbath is His and I for one intend to keep it that way."...

Suddenly there was an interruption.

A uniformed attendant announced, "Lord Lindsay."

Andy hurried in, glanced quickly round, and went and stood by Eric. The Prince and the others gave him friendly looks. Not only was the young Lord one of them, an aristocrat himself, but he had won a silver medal.

"Your Highness, Cadogan, Gentlemen," he said, "I do apologize for barging in like this. The fact is I'm fully aware of Eric's dilemma, and I wonder if I could be so bold as to suggest a possible solution. The 400 meters, it's on Thursday. I've already got my medal, so why don't you let Eric take my place in the 400 meters?"

"I think that's a splendid idea," said the Duke of Sutherland.

Eric turned to Andy.

"Andy, I . . ." It embarassed him that Andy was sacrificing his own chance at another Olympic medal.

Andy grinned. "A pleasure, old chap, just to see you run."

Eric decided he couldn't turn down such a sporting offer. "Then 'Aye' it is." . . .

Lord Birkenhead whispered to the Duke of Sutherland, "Thank God for Lindsay, George. I thought the lad had us beaten."

"He did have us beaten," the Duke said quietly, "And thank God he did."

"I don't follow, George."

"The 'lad,' as you call him, is a true man of principle and a true athlete. His speed is a mere extension of his life, its force. We sought to sever his running from himself."

"For his country's sake."

"No sake is worth that," said the Duke, "Least of all a guilty national pride."

W. J. WEATHERBY, *CHARIOTS OF FIRE* (1981);
BASED ON A SCREENPLAY BY COLIN WELLAND

## The Testing of Convictions

*It is one thing to say, "I believe this is the right action." It is quite another to do the right thing when people oppose us and when doing right seems impossible.*

We need to pass on to our children and remind ourselves that if we have deep convictions—convictions that have not just been handed to us, but that have been seared into our souls through diffcult battles won—those convictions will be tested. They will be tried in the fires of outside pressures. I am not certain that a conviction is a worthwhile one if it is not tested and tried in the refining fires of life experiences and human opposition.

## Integrity Is Threatened By Temptation

*Temptations we face fall into three categories: 1)We are tempted sensually—to inappropriately feed the desires of our physical bodies. 2)We are tempted to presume upon the grace of God—to do things our way, believing God will rescue us. 3)We are tempted in the area of gaining power and control.*

Then Satan tempted him to get food by changing stones into loaves of bread. "It will prove you are the Son of God," he said.

But Jesus told him, "No! For the Scriptures tell us that bread won't feed men's souls: obedience to every word of God is what we need."

Then Satan took him to Jerusalem to the roof of the Temple. "Jump off," he said, "and prove you are the Son of God; for the Scriptures declare, 'God will send his angels to keep you from harm,' . . . they will prevent you from smashing on the rocks below."

Jesus retorted, "It also says not to put the Lord your God to a foolish test!"

Next Satan took him to the peak of a very high mountain and showed him the nations of the world and all their glory. "I'll give it all to you," he said, "if you will only kneel and worship me."

"Get out of here, Satan," Jesus told him. "The Scriptures say, 'Worship only the Lord God. Obey only him.'"

MATTHEW 4:3–10 (TLB), *HOLY BIBLE*

## Standing Against Temptation

*It is not true that people of integrity are not tempted. They are just ready for it and know what to do when it happens. The key is depending on God rather than on their own strength to resist temptation.*

Therefore let him who thinks he stands take heed lest he fall. No temptation has overtaken you but such as is common to man; and God is faithful, who will not allow you to be tempted beyond what you are able, but with the temptation will provide the way of escape also, that you may be able to endure it.

1 CORINTHIANS 10:12–13 (NASB), *HOLY BIBLE*

## An Uphill Climb

*No one says that integrity is easy. Often it is a strain, but in the end it's worth the struggle.*

The hill, though high, I covet to ascend,
The difficult will not me offend;
For I perceive the way to life lies here.
Come, pluck up heart, let's neither faint nor fear;
Better, though difficult, the right way to go,
Then wrong, though easy, where the end is woe.

JOHN BUNYAN, *PILGRIM'S PROGRESS*

*A man of integrity is not one who never does anything wrong, but one who is grieved each time he does and desires to make things right.*

## Integrity Under Pressure

One test of people's character is what they do in hard times—what they do under pressure. Do they compromise their integrity using excuses for their wrong choices? Or do they have the courage to do the right thing no matter what they come up against?

*Bad company corrupts good character.*

1 Corinthians 15:33 (NIV), *Holy Bible*

## Set Your Heart to Do Right

...you don't have to think about doing the right thing. If you're for the right thing, then you do it without thinking.

MAYA ANGELOU, *I KNOW WHY THE CAGED BIRD SINGS* (1969)

## Maintaining Integrity

*This excerpt from a letter dated July 17, 1861, is from a father to his only son, an infantry soldier during the Civil War.*

Try to maintain your Christian profession among your comrades. I need not caution you against strong drink as useless and hurtful, nor against profanity, so common among soldiers. Both these practices you abhor. Aim to take at once a decided stand for God. If practicable have prayers regularly in your tent, or unite with fellow-disciples in prayer-meetings in the camp. Should preaching be accessible, always be a hearer. Let the world know that you are a Christian. Read a chapter in the New Testament, which your mother gave you, every morning and evening, when you can, and engage in secret prayer to God for his holy Spirit to guide and sustain you. I would rather hear of your death than of the shipwreck of your faith and good conscience.

FROM *SOLDIER LIFE* (1882) BY CARLTON MCCARTHY

## Courage to Do Right

*It's easy to go along with what others are doing, and it sometimes feels like the safe thing to do, especially when those "others" are trusted friends. But if we are willing to take a stand for what is right, we can help set a standard for others.*

The judge looked down from his bench and, in a somber voice, declared, "Mr. Wilson, this is your day of reckoning!" Then he sentenced him to seven and one-half years in federal prison.

In response, Wilson's lawyer requested that he be allowed a few minutes with his family and friends before surrendering to the authorities.

The judge replied, "Mr. Wilson is going to be taken by the marshals right now. You should have thought of that before."

Wilson was one of four California men convicted of financial fraud and sentenced to prison in that particular case. Five men were originally investigated, but the fifth, Mark Jacobs, was not arrested and charged.

Jacobs had been invited to join the financial scheme by four friends (the men sent to jail) in a weekly Bible study. They had assured him their plan was totally legal.

Yet something inside him said it wasn't right. While it was hard to say no to good friends, he chose to go with his conscience and tell them he wouldn't participate.

The lawyers for the four convicted men pleaded with the judge that their clients made mistakes of poor judgment. They were good men who loved their wives and kids, gave to charities, and were active in their churches. Their crime involved a "gray" area, crossing a line that wasn't clear.

The judge disagreed. "It is not hard to determine where the line is," he said. "The guy who drew the line is Mark Jacobs. He knew what was right and what was wrong, and he didn't hesitate. Hopefully, now we will have fewer people who are willing to walk up to the line and dabble with going over the line. We will have people like Mr. Jacobs who wouldn't touch this thing with a ten-foot pole."

GARY J. OLIVER, PH.D., IN
*SEVEN PROMISES OF A PROMISEKEEPER* (1994)

*The righteous man walks in his integrity;*
*His children are blessed after him.*

PROVERBS 20:7 (NKJV), *HOLY BIBLE*

*Be advised that every time you avoid doing*
*right, you increase your disposition to do wrong.*

ANONYMOUS

## To Be an Honorable Man

*It's not easy to be a person of honor and integrity.
Those around may not follow suit, and one might have
to stand alone. But doing this will help a person
mature, both mentally and spiritually.*

### If

If you can keep your head when all about you
Are losing theirs and blaming it on you;
If you can trust yourself when all men doubt you,
But make allowance for their doubting too;
If you can wait and not be tired of waiting,
Or, being lied about, don't deal in lies,
Or, being hated, don't give way to hating,
And yet don't look too good, nor talk too wise;

If you can dream—and not make dreams your master;
If you can think—and not make thoughts your aim;
If you can meet with triumph and disaster
And treat these two impostors just the same;
If you can bear to hear the truth you've spoken
Twisted by knaves to make a trap for fools,
Or watch the things you gave your life to broken,
And stoop and build 'em up with wornout tools;

If you can make one heap of all your winnings
And risk it on one turn of pitch-and-toss,
And lose, and start again at your beginnings
And never breathe a word about your loss;
If you can force your heart and nerve and sinew
To serve your turn long after they are gone,
And so hold on when there is nothing in you
Except the Will which says to them: "Hold on";

If you can talk with crowds and keep your virtue,
Or walk with kings—nor lose the common touch;
If neither foes nor loving friends can hurt you;
If all men count with you, but none too much;
If you can fill the unforgiving minute
With sixty seconds' worth of distance run—
Yours is the Earth and everything that's in it,
And which is more—you'll be a Man, my son!

RUDYARD KIPLING

# Character Developed Through Adversity

*When life doesn't go according to our plan, and calamity strikes, our true character is revealed. How we handle adversity signals what kind of person we are deep inside.*

When I think of people I admire, I think of Michael. When he was seventeen, while on a mission trip with the church youth group, he over-rotated a flip while practicing a gymnastics routine and landed on his face. He broke his neck, and he has not taken a step since.

What has amazed me about Michael is his attitude about being in a wheelchair, paralyzed from the chest down with limited use of his hands. When I have seen him at church, I have not heard him complain or give in to self-pity. Instead he always seems to be upbeat and positive. I have not seen him get impatient or lose his temper in frustration as I would at having to ask people for help all the time and having to do things at a slower pace than is normal for such a young person.

"It's not like I don't miss being able to run around," he said to a local newspaper reporter who wrote an article about him when he graduated from St. Petersburg Junior College, after giving a speech from his wheelchair to 800 members of his graduating class. "I miss that, and there are times that I get down, times that I get so fed up, so tired of having to depend on people to do the same old stuff for me over and over."

Lately I'm one of the people that Michael depends on. He has been asking me to go to his house, drive his van down to his college, the University of South Florida, which is about 30 minutes away and bring him home one day a week. I thought I might see the negative side of Michael getting this up close and personal. But I haven't. He didn't even get impatient with me when he had to explain time after time how to correctly connect and tighten the straps that hold his wheelchair securely in place in the van. In fact, each time I drive him home, he cheers and encourages me and my 17-year-old daughter who sometimes comes along. He thinks I'm doing him a favor and helping him out, but some days I wonder who's helping who.

Why is it that someone like Michael can have his character so enriched by adversity while others' lives seem destroyed by it? He claims it is his faith in God. Out of that faith comes his acceptance of his disability—that this is the life God has given him, and he must embrace it and make the best of it. And he is doing just that. He has told his story on television, and he speaks to young people, encouraging them to hang in there. When I asked him recently what his career goals are, he said, "I just want to help people." He's doing that already, in more ways than he knows.

On November 10, 1997, Michael turned 21 years old. An interesting coincidence is that this date was also the 222nd birthday of the United States Marine Corps—an organization that prides itself on looking for "a few good men." Some in society believe that when a male turns twenty-one, he officially reaches manhood. I believe Michael has been a man—a *good* man (God's definition, not the Marines')—for awhile now.

Happy Birthday, Michael!

## A Prayer for Allegiance to God

Deliver me, O God, from a slothful mind, from all lukewarmness, and all dejection of spirit. I know these cannot but deaden my love to you; mercifully free my heart from them, and give me a lively, zealous, active, and cheerful spirit, that I may vigorously perform whatever you command, thankfully suffer whatever you choose for me, and be ever ardent to obey in all things your holy love.

JOHN WESLEY

## People of Integrity Do Soul Searching

*People of high character examine their souls to see if there is anything amiss. Then they take steps to correct the flaws.*

Have you explored your soul? It is not too late to do so. The pursuit is quite rewarding....

It would be a great thing to feel that one had contrived to find out exactly what one's soul is good for; what strains and stresses it can endure; how well equipped it is for the strange adventure upon which it is ultimately to set forth; how fit it is to stand in the white light that beats against the throne of God.

LLOYD C. DOUGLAS, JANUARY 6, 1928,
IN *THE LIVING FAITH* (1955)

*Integrity without knowledge is weak and useless, and knowledge without integrity is dangerous and dreadful.*

SAMUEL JOHNSON (1709–1784)

# Right and Wrong Remain the Same

*Some would like to believe that the times we live in define what is right and what is wrong. There is always evil in any society. People of integrity are able to resist that evil instead of finding ways to call it right and indulging themselves in it.*

They tell us that times have changed, that we live in a new moral climate and must learn to live with it. I also have a conscience and must live with it. Paul lived in an evil day and the spiritual climate was bad. He wrestled with principalities and powers of the world of darkness. He was most concerned to have a good conscience. He is a foolish man who comes to terms with this world at the expense of his soul. We have to live with ourselves and, while everybody is majoring on how to get along with the times, let us remember that we are not thermometers to register the prevailing temperature but thermostats to change it.

VANCE HAVNER, *ALL THE DAYS* (1976)

*Do to others as you would have them do to you.*

Luke 6:31 (NIV), *Holy Bible*

## A Desire to Do Right

*A person of integrity desires to keep God's laws and is willing to be examined by Him. Such a person deliberately seeks out good company.*

I have tried to keep your laws and have trusted you without wavering. Cross-examine me, O Lord, and see that this is so; test my motives and affections too. For I have taken your lovingkindness and your truth as my ideals. I do not have fellowship with tricky, two-faced men; they are false and hypocritical. I hate the sinners' hangouts and refuse to enter them.

Psalm 26:1–5 (TLB), *Holy Bible*

# Peace

*P*eace describes the state of being we all desire to have. The word "peace" brings to mind "the absence of war." It evokes images of people getting along with one another and living together in harmony. A similar sense comes from having inner peace: a quality of internal rest and calm. But neither kind of peace can be had without paying the price for it: We must release everything to God. We know that we've acquired true peace if, when things are chaotic all around us, we can be calm and trust in the One of whom the Scriptures say, "He Himself is our peace . . ."

## Areas of Peace

*God wants us to know peace in every area of our lives—peace in our daily work, our business, our family, our soul. The key to letting peace enter in is to invite God into each of these areas daily.*

Peace in daily work is the consciousness of health and ability to spare so that when one's tasks are done there is a margin all around. Peace in business is the consciousness of capital and plenty, so that one need not fear what the day may bring. Peace in the family is the consciousness that, under all the strains inevitably incident to the running of a home, there is an unfailing wealth of love and devotion and fidelity to fall back upon. Peace in the soul is the consciousness that, however difficult life may be, we are not living it alone . . .

HARRY EMERSON FOSDICK,
*TWELVE TESTS OF CHARACTER* (1923)

# A Heart's Cry for Peace

*We long for peace and an end to all wars. But since we're not in control of this, we must ask God to overtake the world with His peace.*

CHRIST, no one on earth really wants the pain and horror of war. We do not want to kill or to be killed, to hurt or to be hurt. But we all see injustice, and sometimes it makes us angry and we see no other way to right the wrong except by war. Christ, teach us the ways of peace! Calm our angry hearts and grant to all peoples and their leaders unending patience in the search for peace and justice. Help us to be ready to give up some of our comforts and power and pride, so that war will leave the face of the earth and we may work for you in peace.

AVERY BROOKE, *PLAIN PRAYERS IN A COMPLICATED WORLD* (1993)

*Peace—serene confidence, free from fears and agitating passions and moral conflicts.*

2 PETER 3:14 (AMPLIFIED), *HOLY BIBLE*

*If it is possible, as far as it depends on you, live at peace with everyone.*

ROMANS 12:18 (NIV), *HOLY BIBLE*

# Let Go of Anger — Embrace Peace

*One of the greatest peace-robbers in our lives is anger. It affects our minds, our bodies, and our emotions. If we choose to let go of it, we can embrace peace again.*

Lord, I feel angry at so many people. Often I think my life would be peaceful if only they would just do the right thing. I convince myself they are robbing me of peace, but at this moment I know it's *my* choice to let go of anger and embrace peace. Staying angry at them for not living up to my expectations doesn't solve any problems—it just creates new ones. Please help me to remember that "anger does not bring about the righteous life that God desires" (James 1:19, NIV)—in me or in those I'm staying angry at. Give me strength to release them—over and over again if need be—so I can go back to that serene, tranquil place called "peace." In Jesus' name. Amen.

# The World's Way of Seeking Peace

*If we want peace with others, we need to let go of self-interest. Only then does peace become possible.*

Jesus' way would be peace itself if we followed it. But men don't want to change as radically as that! They are still trying to make selfish greed work. In the peace negotiations, nations have jostled for special privilege, and selfish business interests have tried to grab advantages that would be sure to make other men hate them. Senator Vandenberg wrote before the San Francisco Conference that nations were striving for "America first," "England first," "Russia first,"—the very attitude which has caused all wars. Peace cannot be permanent until we put "the whole world first." No part of the world, whether America or England or Russia, or any business enterprise, is as important as the welfare of all. "Thy kingdom come on earth" is not only Christian, it is the only possible road to lasting peace.

FRANK C. LAUBACH, *PRAYER: THE MIGHTIEST FORCE IN THE WORLD* (1946)

*Blessed are the peacemakers: for they shall be called the children of God.*

MATTHEW 5:9 (KJV), *HOLY BIBLE*

## Becoming a Peacemaker

*Can we find peace in a pill or in therapy? Or is it true that peace comes from God alone?*

Where does peacemaking begin? How can we become peacemakers?

We have pointed out that peace can never come out of war. War is the sire of poverty, depression, suffering, and hatred—it has never given us permanent peace.

Can peace be discovered within ourselves? Freud has told us that peace is but a mental attitude. Cast off our phobias, shed our neuroses, and "bingo!"—we'll have the coveted peace men long for.

I respect psychiatry for what it can do. Unquestionably it has helped many. But it certainly is no satisfactory substitute for the peace which can only come from God. If psychiatry leaves God out, ultimately we shall see psychiatrists going to each other for treatment. There can be no peace until we find peace with God.

BILLY GRAHAM, *THE SECRET OF HAPPINESS* (1955)

*When a man's ways are pleasing to the LORD, he makes even his enemies live at peace with him.*

PROVERBS 16:7 (NIV), *HOLY BIBLE*

## Love and Peace

*Do we really want peace the way God views peace? Perhaps we need to rethink our idea of what "peace" really is. God is always ready to give us true peace, if we are willing to ask Him for it.*

Will you end wars by asking men to trust men who evidently cannot be trusted? No. Teach them to love and trust God; then they will be able to love the men they cannot trust, and will dare to make peace with them, not trusting in them but in God....

Perhaps peace is not, after all, something you work for, or "fight for." It is indeed "fighting for peace" that starts all the wars.... Peace is something you have or you do not have. If you are yourself at peace, then there is at least *some* peace in the world. Then share your peace with everyone, and everyone will be at peace.

THOMAS MERTON, *THE TRUE SOLITUDE* (1969)

*Peace hath her victories No less renowned than War.*

JOHN MILTON, *TO THE LORD GENERAL CROMWELL* (1652)

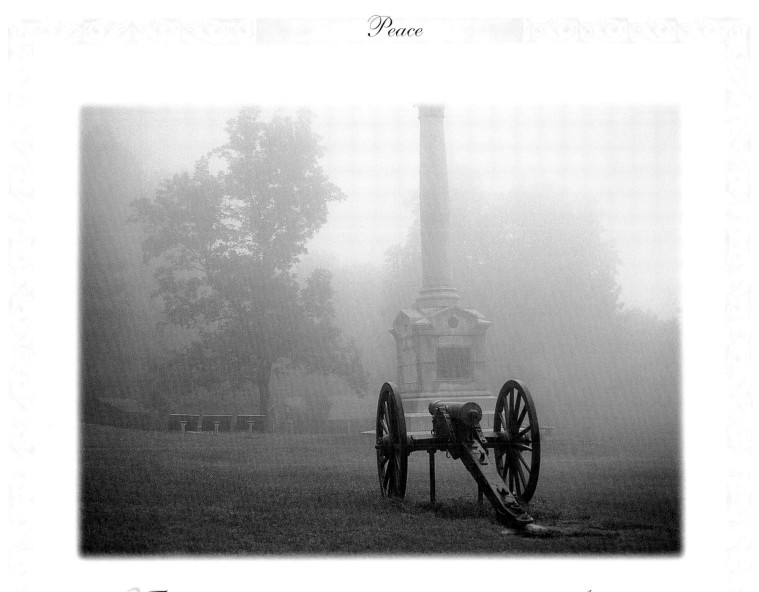

*There is an appointed time for everything. And there is a time for every event under heaven . . . A time for war, and a time for peace.* ECCLESIASTES 3:1, 8 (NASB), *HOLY BIBLE*

## Peaceful Thoughts

*When we focus on the negative, peace eludes us. But positive thinking leads to peace.*

Fix your thoughts on what is true and good and right. Think about things that are pure and lovely, and dwell on the fine, good things in others. Think about all you can praise God for and be glad about. Keep putting into practice all you learned from me and saw me doing, and the God of peace will be with you.

PHILIPPIANS 4:8–9 (TLB), *HOLY BIBLE*

## Prayer Brings Peace

*Instead of lugging around our cares, we can pray. Prayer opens the door to peace.*

Don't worry about anything; instead, pray about everything; tell God your needs and don't forget to thank him for his answers. If you do this you will experience God's peace, which is far more wonderful than the human mind can understand. His peace will keep your thoughts and your hearts quiet and at rest as you trust in Christ Jesus.

PHILIPPIANS 4:6–7 (TLB), *HOLY BIBLE*

## Peace Is Declared

*The soul celebrates when a war ends, whether on the battlefield, in our homes, or on the job. At those times, peace seems like a brand-new, lovely thing.*

The cries sound gradually fainter. The road drags on toilsomely. We are carrying a lot of stuff—a man must bring something back home with him. Clouds hang in the sky. During the afternoon the sun breaks through, and birch trees, now with only a few leaves left, hang mirrored in puddles of rain along the way. Soft blue haze is caught in the branches.

As I march on with pack and lowered head, by the side of the road I see an image of bright, silken trees reflected in the pools of rain. In the occasional mirrors they are displayed clearer than in reality. They get another

light and in another way. Embedded there in the brown earth lies a span of sky, trees, depths and clearness. Suddenly I shiver. For the first time in many years I feel again that something is still beautiful, that this in all its simplicity is beautiful and pure, this image in the water pool before me—and in this thrill my heart leaps up. For a moment all that other falls away, and now, for the first time, I feel it; I see it; I comprehend it fully: Peace. The weight that nothing eased before now lifts at last. Something strange, something new flies up, a dove—a white dove. Trembling horizon, tremulous expectancy, first glimpse, presentiment, hope, exaltation, imminence: Peace.

Sudden panic, and I look around. There behind me on the stretchers my comrades are now lying and still they call. It is peace, yet they must die. But I, I am trembling with joy and am not ashamed.—And that is odd.

Because none can ever wholly feel what another suffers—is that the reason why wars perpetually recur?

Erich Maria Remarque, <small>The Road Back</small> (1931);
Translated from German by A. W. Wheen

## With Acceptance Comes Peace

*We can decide to be at peace with the state of our lives. If we're constantly desiring more and better things and positions, rather than being contented with what we have, we'll never know true peace.*

To enjoy a little happiness, to have a taste of heaven on earth, you must accept life, your own life, just as it is now. You must be at peace with your work, with the people around you, with their faults and their imperfections. You must be content with your husband, your wife, even if you now realize you did not marry the ideal husband or the ideal wife. (I don't believe they exist anyway.) You must be at peace with the size of your purse, your status in the community, with your face (which you did not choose yourself), with your home, your furniture, your clothes, with your own living standards—even if your neighbor's things are so much better and so much finer, so you think. Accept life. You only have one skin. You can't be born again in another one.

PHIL BOSMANS, *GIVE HAPPINESS A CHANCE* (1980)

## The LORD blesses His people with peace.

PSALM 29:11 (NIV), *HOLY BIBLE*

## A Place to Find Peace

*Sometimes we find a place where we can go and find peace. We listen to the sounds of nature and observe the beauty of God's creation, and we know He is still in control.*

This is my ledge
of quiet,
my shelf of peace,
edged
by its crooked rails
holding back the beyond.
Above,
a hawk sails
high
to challenge clouds
trespassing
my plot of sky.
Below,
in the valley,
remote and dim,

sounds
come and go,
a requiem
for quiet.
Here on my ledge,
quiet praise:
of birds,
crickets,
breeze —
in different ways;
and so do I —
for these:
my ledge of quiet,
my plot of sky:
for peace.

RUTH BELL GRAHAM, *SITTING BY MY LAUGHING FIRE...* (1977)

## Peace in the Midst of Tragedy

*Sometimes we believe our souls can only be at peace if there is no outer turmoil. The wonder of God's peace is that even when the world around us is in confusion and our emotions are in a whirl, underneath it all we can know His peace.*

When Mr. Moody and I were holding meetings in Edinburg, in 1874, we heard the sad news of the loss of the French steamer, "Ville De Havre," on her return from America to France, with a large number of members of the Ecumenical Council whose meetings had been held in Philadelphia. On board the steamer was a Mrs. Spafford, with her four children. In mid-ocean a collision took place with a large sailing vessel, causing the steamer to sink in half an hour. Nearly all on board were lost. Mrs. Spafford got her children out of their berths and up on deck. On being told that the vessel would soon sink, she knelt down with her children in prayer, asking God that they might be saved if possible; or be made willing to die, if that was his will. In a few minutes the vessel sank to the bottom of the sea, and the children were lost. One of the sailors of the vessel, named Lockurn—whom I afterward met in Scotland—while rowing over the spot where the vessel disappeared, discovered Mrs. Spafford floating in the water. Ten days later she was landed at Cardiff, Wales. From there she cabled to her husband, a lawyer in Chicago, the message, "Saved alone." Mr. Spafford, who was a Christian, had the message framed and hung up in his office. He started immediately for England to bring his wife to Chicago. Mr. Moody left his meeting in Edinburgh and went to Liverpool to try to comfort the bereaved parents, and was greatly pleased to find that they were able to say: "It is well; the will of God be done."

In 1876, when we returned to Chicago to work, I was entertained at the home of Mr. and Mrs. Spafford for a number of weeks. During that time Mr. Spafford wrote the hymn, "It is well with my soul," in commemoration of the death of his children.

IRA D. SANKEY, *SANKEY'S STORY OF THE GOSPEL HYMNS* (1906)

## It Is Well With My Soul

When peace, like a river, attendeth my way.
When sorrows like sea billows roll;
Whatever my lot, thou hast taught me to say,
It is well, it is well with my soul.
It is well with my soul, it is well, it is well with my soul.

HORATIO G. SPAFFORD

*Peace I leave with you: my peace I give to you; not as the world gives do I give to you. Let not your hearts be troubled, neither let them be afraid.*

JOHN 14:27 (RSV), *HOLY BIBLE*

## Reflections on Peace

*We all make plans for our lives and have an agenda we want to hold on to. Yet if we let go and let God be in charge, the result will bring us peace.*

Peace is about releasing.
It's about opening my hand
and letting go of my plan,
my agenda, my demands
on God and other people
and even on myself.
It's about realizing
that every person
is as important as I am
in God's eyes.
It's remembering
I don't know everything
and I don't have solutions
to every problem.
It's about calling on
the One who does.

## Prayer for Peace

*When life's demands press in on us and we are weary in body and mind, we can call out to God for His peace.*

Lord Jesus, as we pray for the Members of this body, its officers, and all those who share in its labors, we remember that Thou wert never in a hurry and never lost Thine inner peace even under pressure greater than we shall ever know.

But we are only human.
We grow tired.

We feel the strain of meeting deadlines, and we chafe under frustration.

We need poise and peace of mind, and only Thou canst supply the deepest needs of tired bodies, jaded spirits, and frayed nerves.

Give to us Thy peace and refresh us in our weariness, that this may be a good day with much done and done well, that we may say with Thy servant Paul, "I can do all things through Christ, who gives me strength." AMEN.

PRAYER PRAYED ON JUNE 12, 1948, BEFORE THE U.S. SENATE BY CHAPLAIN FOR THE U.S. SENATE, PETER MARSHALL; FROM *A MAN CALLED PETER* BY CATHERINE MARSHALL

# Kindness

We've all heard that "actions speak louder than words." And so it is with the Christian life. Like it or not, we affect others by what we say and do. The Bible admonishes us to "Never tire of loyalty and kindness. Hold these virtues tightly" (Proverbs 3:3, TLB). As examples in "word and deed" we are instructed to "...clothe yourselves with compassion, kindness, humility, gentleness and patience" (Colossians 3:12, NIV). Whether with friends, family, coworkers, or even total strangers, God wants us to always treat others with the utmost care and respect.

*Since God chose you to be the holy people whom he loves, you must clothe yourselves with tenderhearted mercy, kindness, humility, gentleness, and patience.*

COLOSSIANS 3:12 (NLT), *HOLY BIBLE*

## A Little Word

A little word in kindness spoken,
    A motion or a tear,
Has often healed the heart that's broken!
    And made a friend sincere.

A word—a look—has crushed to earth,
    Full many a budding flower,
Which had a smile but owned its birth,
    Would bless life's darkest hour.

Then deem it not an idle thing,
    A pleasant work to speak;
The face you wear, the thoughts you bring,
    A heart may heal or break.

AUTHOR UNKNOWN

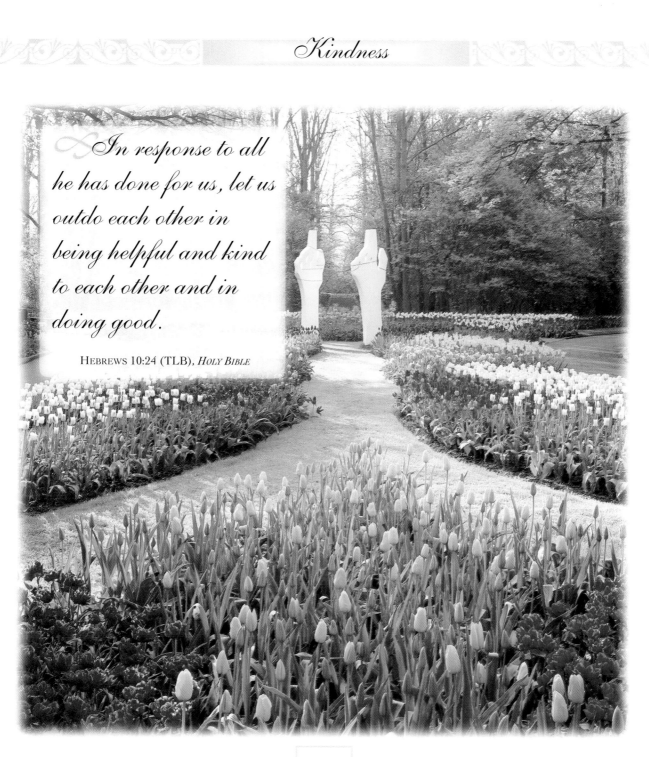

*In response to all he has done for us, let us outdo each other in being helpful and kind to each other and in doing good.*

HEBREWS 10:24 (TLB), *HOLY BIBLE*

## Spontaneous Kindness

Always, Sir, set a high value on spontaneous kindness. He whose inclination prompts him to cultivate your friendship of his own accord will love you more than one whom you have been at pains to attach to you.

SAMUEL JOHNSON (1709–1784)

## Kindness

Show a little kindness —
 Help a brother on the way.
Show a little kindness —
 In all you do and say.
Show a little kindness —
 it will soon come back to you,
As everyone around you
 starts showing kindness, too!

## Rules of Conduct

Do all the good you can,
By all the means you can,
In all the ways you can,
In all the places you can,
At all the times you can,
To all the people you can,
As long as ever you can.

JOHN WESLEY (1915)

# I Shall Not Pass This Way Again

*We often do not get a second chance for doing the good deed that we should have done, but neglected to do, in the first place. So if you see the chance to do something good—do it now!*

Through this toilsome world, alas!
Once and only once I pass;
If a kindness I may show,
If a good deed I may do
To a suffering fellow man,
Let me do it while I can.
No delay, for it is plain
I shall not pass this way again.

AUTHOR UNKNOWN

# Too Kind!

I have wept in the night
For the shortness of sight
    That to somebody's need made me blind.
But I never have yet
Felt a tinge of regret
    For being a little too kind!

AUTHOR UNKNOWN

# Act Kindly

*When our lives are changed by God's mercy, we are expected to show this same mercy in our dealings with others.*

Talk and act like a person expecting to be judged by the Rule that sets us free. For if you refuse to act kindly, you can hardly expect to be treated kindly. Kind mercy wins over harsh judgment every time.

JAMES 2:12–14 (THE MESSAGE), *HOLY BIBLE*

## Simple Act of Kindness

*Just one seemingly simple act of kindness can have far-reaching consequences. If we stop to help someone out, we might make their day—or even make a new friend.*

It was late Saturday afternoon when the pleasant-looking young lady with shoulder-length chestnut hair caught my attention—or rather the ankle-to-knee purple wrap over her leg cast caught it.

She was walking slowly on her crutches down the sloping sidewalk leading to the post office.

I flashed a smile toward her as I reached for my car door, "That looks like a real pain," I called to her.

"You're right, it is," she chuckled. Then, reaching the bench in front of my car, she called back, "You wouldn't happen to have change for a $10 bill would you? I need to buy stamps from the machine."

"No, sorry. I only have a $20," I replied as I closed the door and put my key in the ignition.

"Oh well, I'll just sit here until someone comes along."

*Stop. Elaine, you dummy. What's keeping you from running across the street to get change for her?* The message came emblazoned across my conscience.

She was shocked to see me reopen the car door and walk toward her. "I'll be happy to run and get change for you from the grocery store."

"Oh, you don't have to do that. Someone will probably come with change pretty soon," she replied.

"I'd like to, really...it'll just take a minute. Wait a minute. Let me check the machine, first."

It took only three quick steps to reach the Post Office door and see the big "Out of Order" sign taped to the stamp dispenser. "Sorry, but there are no stamps here. The machine is out of order again."

In the next couple of minutes we brainstormed other possibilities. But on our little Northwest island, there appeared to be no other place to buy stamps.

*Wait, Elaine. What's wrong with looking in your purse and giving her yours?* There it was again—the still, small voice.

She was still talking to me, "That figures. I've had nothing but bad luck since I moved here. I nearly froze to death in our winter storm. My landlord was in California and I had no water or electricity. Then I had this accident and now I can't even drive to get around for another forty-five days. My psychic told me this was my unlucky line and I shouldn't live in the Northwest. And the whole country is so militaristic. People here are unfriendly. I'd better just move to another country."

I breathed a quick prayer for just the right words to respond to her. "Just a minute," I broke in. "I have stamps in my purse in the car. Let me get them so you can mail the letters that you need to today."

"I have 29 cents in change. I can buy one from you. Oh, and here's my lucky silver dollar. You can take that, too," she said.

"No. I don't need your money. Here—take three or four extra," I insisted as I tore several from the little book of stamps I'd retrieved from my car.

We chatted for a few more minutes and I learned she lived less than a mile from me. She had also become a volunteer cat and dog walker at the Humane Society to help alleviate her loneliness.

*Give her your business card.* There it was again—the still, small voice. I was getting more involved than I planned. Quickly I went back to the car and got the card with my phone number.

"Listen, Denise (now I knew her name), I live near you. Give me a call if you need a ride to town. I come in at least twice a day and I'd be happy to swing by and pick you up."

By this time she was reading my business card…Christian Writers Consultant, it said under my name. "Oh! No wonder—you're a Christian. The only other person to be nice to me this week was a Christian, Rev. Baker, pastor at the Baptist church."

Sitting on the bench beside her, my schedule no longer seemed to matter as much as this lonely new neighbor. I was genuinely interested in her, her background, and her travels around the world. We talked another twenty minutes before I really had to go.

"I'll call you. Can we get together next week?" she asked when I stood to leave.

"Of course," I said. And as I drove away, I was smiling, not just at her but with deep thankfulness for that still, small voice.

## Kindness and Compassion: In God's Words

Luke 6:35 (NIV) — But love your enemies, do good to them, and lend to them without expecting to get anything back. Then your reward will be great, and you will be sons of the most high, because he is kind to the ungrateful and wicked.

1 Peter 2:3 (TLB) — Now that you realize how kind the Lord has been to you . . .

Ephesians 4:32 (NIV) — Be kind and compassionate to one another, forgiving each other, just as in Christ God forgave you.

Romans 2:4 (NIV) — Do you show contempt for the riches of his kindness, tolerance and patience, not realizing that God's kindness leads you toward repentance?

Ephesians 2:7 (TLB) — And now God can always point to us as examples of how very, very rich his kindness is, as shown in all he has done for us through Christ Jesus.

2 Corinthians 6:6 (TLB) — We have proved ourselves to be what we claim by our wholesome lives and by our understanding of the Gospel and by our patience. We have been kind and truly loving and filled with the Holy Spirit.

1 Corinthians 13:4 (NIV) — Love is patient, love is kind. It does not envy, it does not boast, it is not proud.

Galatians 5:22–23 (TLB) — But when the Holy Spirit controls our lives he will produce this kind of fruit in us: love, joy, peace, patience, kindness, goodness, faithfulness, gentleness and self-control . . .

## Tender Hearts and Humble Minds

*In God's Kingdom, revenge is unacceptable. Therefore, we are admonished to pray for people rather than to insult, pay back, or get even with them.*

Finally, all of you should be of one mind, full of sympathy toward each other, loving one another with tender hearts and humble minds. Don't repay evil for evil. Don't retaliate when people say unkind things about you. Instead, pay them back with a blessing. That is what God wants you to do, and he will bless you for it.

1 Peter 3:8–9 (NLT), Holy Bible

A friend is a person with whom I may be sincere. Before him I may think aloud.

A friend is the first person who comes in when the whole world has gone out.

RALPH WALDO EMERSON

*Treat your friends for what you know them to be. Regard no surfaces. Consider not what they did but what they intended.*

HENRY DAVID THOREAU

*We ought to help one another by our advice, and yet more by our good examples.*

BROTHER LAWRENCE,
*THE PRACTICE OF THE PRESENCE OF GOD* (1958)

# Pass It On

*The best way to increase the happiness of ourselves and others is by spreading it around.*

Have you had a kindness shown? Pass it on, Pass it on!
'Twas not given for thee alone, Pass it on, pass it on!
Let it travel down the years, Let it wipe another's tears;
Till in heav'n the deed appears, Pass it on, pass it on!

Did you hear the loving word! Pass it on, Pass it on!
Like the singing of a bird? Pass it on, pass it on!
Let its music live and grow, Let it cheer another's woe;
You have reaped what others sow, Pass it on, pass it on!

Have you found the heav'nly light? Pass it on, Pass it on!
Souls are groping in the night, Daylight gone, daylight gone!
Hold your lighted lamp on high, Be a star in someone's sky,
He may live who else would die, Pass it on, pass it on!

Chorus:
Pass it on, pass it on!
Cheerful word or loving deed, Pass it on,
Live for self, you live in vain;
Live for Christ, you live again,
Live for him, with him you reign,
Pass it on, pass it on!

WM. J. KIRKPATRICK (1888)

*The Lord is gracious, and full of compassion; slow to anger, and of great mercy.* PSALM 145:8 (KJV), *HOLY BIBLE*

## Compassionate Listening

Are we tuning out
or tuning in—
what are our habits
of listening?
Do we really care
to share a part
when a troubled sister
bares her heart?
Do words rush out
when nothing should be said—
when all we should do
is listen instead?

*A friend is always loyal, and a brother is born to help in time of need.*

PROVERBS 17:17 (NLT), *HOLY BIBLE*

*So then whatever you desire that others would do to and for you, even so do you also to and for them, for this sums up the Law and the prophets.*

MATTHEW 7:12 (AMPLIFIED), *HOLY BIBLE*

*Remember that none of us has a responsibility to care for the whole world. Instead, our task is to care for the people who are closest to us. In this way we care for the world by starting with individuals, one at a time.*

GARY R. COLLINS, *THE JOY OF CARING* (1980)

## A Helping Heart

If I can stop one Heart from breaking
    I shall not live in vain;
If I can ease one life the aching,
    Or cool one pain,
Or help one fainting robin
    Into his nest again,
I shall not live in vain.

EMILY DICKINSON (1830–1886)

## Just One Need at a Time

*"He will encourage the fainthearted, those tempted to despair. He will see full justice given to all who have been wronged. He won't be satisfied until truth and righteousness prevail throughout the earth…" (Isaiah 42:3-4, TLB).*

God,
I look around my community today
and I feel helpless.
The homeless, the hurting,
the needs each one represents
are more than I can handle.
But
You can do it.
You can meet each need.
Teach me.
Strengthen me and
use me to serve
as I reach out
to my neighbor
and meet
Just One Need at a Time!

## Opportunities Don't Wait

*Seize the opportunity—it may never come again. Today's the day to reach out and lend a helping hand.*

Can't you see she's floundering—
your plans will surely wait.
If you don't offer help now,
tomorrow may be too late.

Sure—it's not convenient,
interruptions never are.
But when you stop to help another,
life is happier by far.

Love is very patient and kind, never jealous or envious, never boastful or proud, never haughty or selfish or rude. Love does not demand its own way. It is not irritable or touchy. It does not hold grudges and will hardly even notice when others do it wrong. It is never glad about injustice, but rejoices whenever truth wins out.

1 Corinthians 13:4–6 (TLB), *Holy Bible*

## Please Let Me Help You

*"It is God himself who has made us what we are and given us new lives from Christ Jesus; and long ages ago he planned that we should spend these lives in helping others" (Ephesians 2:10, TLB).*

Please let me help you
however I can.
Long ages ago
it was God's plan
for me to serve,
to love and to share —
helping ease another's
burden of care.
So let me be
God's loving gift to you
because in serving others,
I am blessed, too.

*Do not forget or neglect to do kindness and good, to be generous and distribute and contribute to the needy [of the church as embodiment and proof of fellowship], for such sacrifices are well-pleasing to God.*

HEBREWS 13:16 (AMPLIFIED), *HOLY BIBLE*

## Take the Risk of Reaching Out

Often when we feel lonely or depressed, the best way to feel better is to give of ourselves. Not only will our own mood improve, but we'll lift someone else's spirit, too!

It's well-known that Seattle gets a lot of rain. Rain, clouds, and the normal dark, miserable days tend to bring out my winter doldrums. Then it is easy to get preoccupied with "how I feel," "wish I had enough money to go find sun in Hawaii," "what's there to do in the rain," etc.

Shortly after moving to Seattle and not yet used to the long rainy season, I soon became tired of myself and my pity party. Looking for a book out of my library to bury myself in, I was inspired by these words from Charles Swindoll:

That's right, give some of yourself away.

Give an hour of your time to someone who needs you.
Give a note of encouragement to someone who is down.
Give a hug of affirmation to someone in your family.
Give a visit of mercy to someone who is laid aside.
Give a meal you prepared to someone who is sick.
Give a word of compassion to someone who just lost a mate.
Give a deed of kindness to someone who is slow and easily overlooked.
Jesus taught: "... to the extent that you did it to one of these brothers of Mine, even the least of them, you did it to Me" (Matthew 25:40, NAS).

The challenge was too obvious. It was true that the most meaningful experiences of my life had come when I dared to risk and reach out to others. When I am touching, smiling, helping, giving, and reaching beyond myself, I come much closer to being the person that God designed me to be.

*Thus speaketh the LORD of hosts, saying, Execute true judgment, and show mercy and compassions every man to his brother: And oppress not the widow, nor the fatherless, the stranger, nor the poor; and let none of you imagine evil against his brother in your heart.*

ZECHARIAH 7:9–10 (KJV), *HOLY BIBLE*

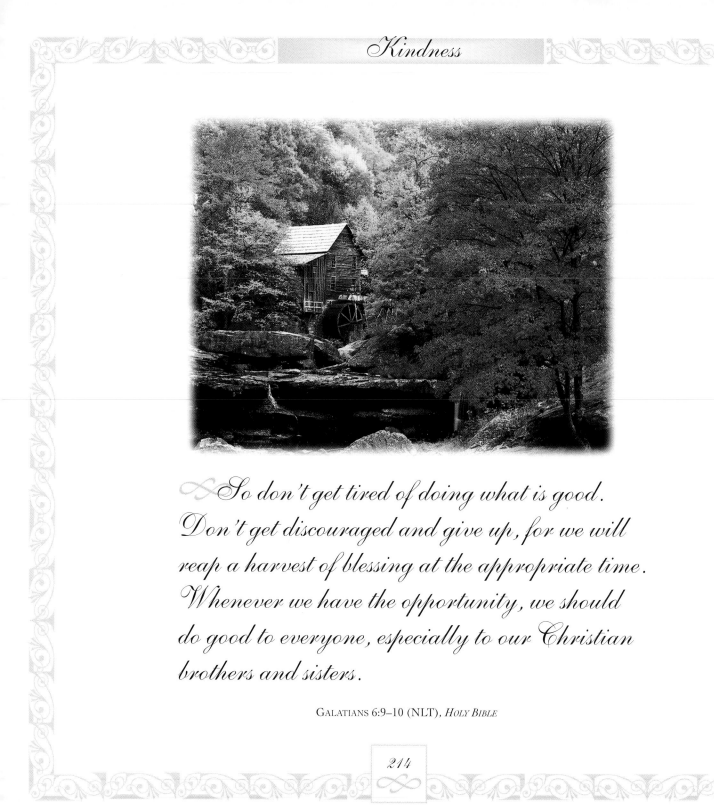

*So don't get tired of doing what is good. Don't get discouraged and give up, for we will reap a harvest of blessing at the appropriate time. Whenever we have the opportunity, we should do good to everyone, especially to our Christian brothers and sisters.*

GALATIANS 6:9–10 (NLT), *HOLY BIBLE*

# What Does It Mean to Care?

*Of all the things that caring implies, often what matters most is simply our presence.*

What does it mean to care? Let me start by saying that the word *care* has become a very ambivalent word. When someone says: "I will take care of him!" it is more likely an announcement of an impending attack than of a tender compassion. . . . The basic meaning of care is: to grieve, to experience sorrow, to cry out with. I am very much struck by this background of the word *care* because we tend to look at caring as an attitude of the strong toward the weak, of the powerful toward the powerless, of the have's toward the have not's. And, in fact, we feel quite uncomfortable with an invitation to enter into someone's pain before doing something about it.

Still, when we honestly ask ourselves which persons in our lives mean the most to us, we often find that it is those who, instead of giving much advice, solutions, or cures, have chosen rather to share our pain and touch our wounds with a gentle and tender hand. The friend who can be silent with us in a moment of despair or confusion, who can stay with us in an hour of grief and bereavement, who can tolerate not-knowing, not-curing, not-healing and face with us the reality of our powerlessness, that is the friend who cares.

You might remember moments in which you were called to be with a friend who had lost a wife or husband, child or parent. What can you say, do, or propose at such a moment? There is a strong inclination to say: "Don't cry; the one you loved is in the hands of God." "Don't be sad because there are so many good things left worth living for." But are we ready to really experience our powerlessness in the face of death and say: "I do not understand. I do not know what to do but I am here with you." Are we willing to **not** run away from the pain, to **not** get busy when there is nothing to do and instead stand rather in the face of death together with those who grieve?

The friend who cares makes it clear that whatever happens in the external world, being present to each other is what really matters

HENRI J. M. NOUWEN, *OUT OF SOLITUDE* (1974)

## The Tie That Binds

*The following story is told about the origin of the beloved hymn "Blest Be the Tie That Binds." It's a reminder that being close to loved ones can be more important than material riches.*

In 1772, after a few years in pastoral work, the Rev. John Fawcett, an English Baptist, was called to London to succeed the famous Dr. Gill. His farewell sermon had been preached in his country church in Yorkshire. The wagons stood loaded with his furniture and books. All was ready for the family's departure.

But his loving congregation were heartbroken. Men, women, and children with sadness and tears gathered around the wagon. Others, sobbing, clung to him and his family.

Finally, overwhelmed with the sorrow of those they were leaving, Dr. Fawcett and his wife sat down on one of the packing cases and they, too, cried.

"Oh, John!" cried Mrs. Fawcett at last. "I cannot bear this! I know not how I can leave these dear friends. How will I be able to go?"

"Nor can I, either," replied her husband. "And we will not go. The wagons shall be unloaded, and everything returned to its old place."

The friends that had gathered were filled with intense joy and gratitude at this turn of events.

Dr. Fawcett at once sent a letter to London explaining their decision, and then resolutely returned to his work on his pitifully small salary.

This hymn was written to commemorate the event. So universal are the sentiments it expresses that it has become one of our hymns immortal.

## Blest Be the Tie That Binds

*Friends and family members are often
separated by distance. But we know that God
is the tie that binds us all together, no matter
where we are.*

Blest be the tie that binds
Our hearts in Christian love;
The fellowship of kindred minds
Is like to that above.

Before our Father's throne
We pour our ardent pray'rs;
Our fears, our hopes, our aims are one —
Our comforts and our cares.

When we asunder part
It gives us inward pain,
But we shall still be joined in heart,
And hope to meet again.

REV. JOHN FAWCETT

## Kindness Fills the Heart With Joy

We cannot tell the precise moment
when friendship is formed. As in
filling a vessel drop by drop, there is
at last a drop which makes it run over,
so in a series of kindnesses there is at
last one that makes the heart run over.

SAMUEL JOHNSON (1709–1784)

217

*When friendships are real, they are not glass threads, or frostwork, but the solidest thing we know.*

RALPH WALDO EMERSON

*Go often to the house of thy friend, for weeds choke up the unused path.*

SCANDINAVIAN EDDA

*If you love someone you will be loyal to him no matter what the cost. You will always believe in him, always expect the best of him, and always stand your ground in defending him.*

1 Corinthians 13:7 (TLB), *Holy Bible*

*Oh, the comfort—the inexpressible comfort of feeling safe with a person—having neither to weigh thoughts nor measure words, but pouring them all right out, just as they are, chaff and grain together; certain that a faithful hand will take them and sift them, keep what is worth keeping, and then with the breath of kindness blow the rest away.*

Dinah Maria Mulock Craik

## Then, Let Us Pray

*It's amazing, yet true, that often—at the very time of our desperate need—God, through the Holy Spirit, has led someone to intercede on our behalf.*

The day was long, the burden I had borne
    Seemed heavier that I could longer bear;
And then it lifted—but I did not know
    Someone had knelt in prayer.

Had taken me to God that very hour,
    And asked the easing of the load, and He
In infinite compassion, had stooped down
    And lifted the burden from me.

We cannot tell how often as we pray
    For some bewildered one, hurt and distressed,
The answer comes, but many times these hearts
    Find sudden peace and rest.

Someone had prayed, and faith, a lifted hand
    Reached up to God, and He reached down that day.
So many, many hearts have need of prayer—
    Then, let us, let us pray.

AUTHOR UNKNOWN

*To be a friend you must be there—encouraging, cheering, empathizing, crying. It's all part of the package of friendship.*

# Pray for One Another

*People can often sense when someone is in need of prayer—even if that someone is miles away. If the thought of a friend should come into your mind, why not stop a say a little prayer on their behalf?*

I cannot tell why there should come to me
    A thought of someone miles and miles away,
In swift insistence on the memory,
    Unless a need there be that I should pray.

Too hurried oft are we to spare the thought
    For days together, of some friend away;
Perhaps God does it for us, and we ought
    To read this signal as a call to pray.

Perhaps, just then, my friend has fiercer fight
    And more appalling weakness, and decay
Of courage, darkness, some lost sense of right
    And so in case he needs my prayer, I pray.

Friend, do the same for me. If I intrude
    Unasked upon you, on some crowded day,
Give me a moment's prayer as interlude;
    Be very sure I need it; therefore pray.

MARIANNE FARNINGHAM

## Friendship

Friendship—
a fleeting thing
that comes and goes.
What makes it last,
the magic ingredient?
Nobody knows!
Charisma, interest,
need, and caring,
human involvement,
loving, sharing,
a smile, a card,
friendship to see,
loving a person,
and letting them be,
remembering, talking,
baring your heart,
complex and simple
many things share a part.
Friendship is more than emotion.
Friendships are here to stay.
If we want to have more friends,
we must give more love away.

*Love forgets mistakes;*
*nagging about them parts*
*the best of friends.*

PROVERBS 17:9 (TLB), *HOLY BIBLE*

# What a Friend Does

*Experts have long known the value of friendships. The billion-dollar greeting card industry, as well as various poems, books, and songs, all extol the value of friendship.*

A friend affirms the worth of another individual: (1) by letting them know they are loved and appreciated just as they are; (2) by not trying to lead them to make changes to fit into a particular mold, but allowing them to be unique; (3) by helping them discover their God-given talents and abilities and providing opportunities where these gifts can be used and grow. It is with friends that we test our self-worth in the world.

Your best friend believes in you enough to enable you to go out and act upon your dreams and desires, so that you are finally able to believe in yourself. Friendships help keep us healthy—physically, mentally, and spiritually. A friend does not always have all the answers, but will go with you to God to hear from Him.

# Becoming a Friend

*It takes work to be the helpful, considerate, caring person that others will want to know and spend time with, but it is well worth the investment.*

Being a friend means that you need to reach out. Is there someone you can think of who needs to know that you are there for them—that you are a friend who cares? Pray for the spirit of friendship to so light up your life that you'll radiate this brightness to someone who needs you.

"Dear God, shine through me and help me lighten another's darkness by showing the same friendship that you extended. Show me a person that is in desperate need of a friend today. Help me to be sensitive, caring, and willing to go out of my way to meet this person's need right now, whether it be emotional, physical, or spiritual. Thank you that when I need a friend, YOU are 'the friend that sticketh closer than a brother.' In Jesus' name, Amen."

The stars come nightly to the sky;
The tidal wave unto the sea;
Nor time, nor space, nor deep, nor high
Can keep my own away from me.
Friendship is the triple alliance of the three great
      powers, Love, Sympathy, and Help.
My friends have come to me unsought; the great
      God gave them to me.

RALPH WALDO EMERSON

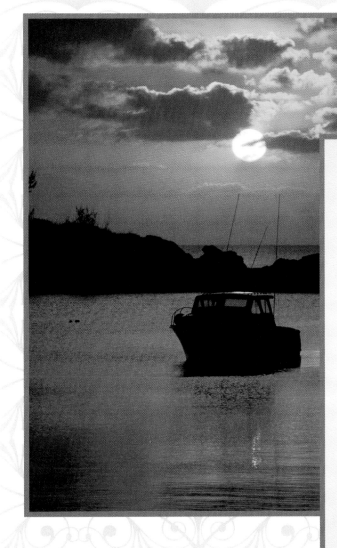

# Service

To serve means to assist or be of use. Serving is one of the reasons we are on this earth and the reason Jesus himself said He came to earth. When we serve, we reach out to meet the needs of others; service is an outward sign that we belong to God and desire to do His will. True service is not about grudgingly doing for others because of obligation, but an act that flows willingly, as a channel for God's love. True servants give not just with their hands, but with their hearts.

# A Humble Servant

*Jesus washed His disciples' feet as an example of how to be a humble servant to others.*

Just before the Passover Feast, Jesus knew that the time had come to leave this world to go to the Father. Having loved his dear companions, he continued to love them right to the end. It was suppertime. The Devil by now had Judas, son of Simon the Iscariot, firmly in his grip, all set for the betrayal.

Jesus knew that the Father had put him in complete charge of everything, that he came from God and was on his way back to God. So he got up from the supper table, set aside his robe, and put on an apron. Then he poured water into a basin and began to wash the feet of the disciples, drying them with an apron. When he got to Simon Peter, Peter said, "Master, you wash my feet?"

Jesus answered, "You don't understand now what I'm doing, but it will be clear enough to you later."

Peter persisted, "You're not going to wash my feet—ever!"

Jesus said, "If I don't wash you, you can't be part of what I'm doing."

"Master!" said Peter. "Not only my feet, then. Wash my hands! Wash my head!"

Jesus said, "If you've had a bath in the morning, you only need your feet washed now and you're clean from head to toe. My concern, you understand, is holiness, not hygiene. So now you're clean. But not every one of you." (He knew who was betraying him. That's why he said, "Not every one of you.") After he had finished washing their feet, he took his robe, put it back on, and went back to his place at the table.

Then he said, "Do you understand what I have done to you? You address me as 'Teacher' and 'Master' and rightly so. That is what I am. So if I, the Master and Teacher, washed your feet, you must now wash each other's feet. I've laid down a pattern for you. What I've done, you do. I'm only pointing out the obvious. A servant is not ranked above his master; an employee doesn't give orders to the employer. If you understand what I'm telling you, act like it—live a blessed life."

JOHN 13:4–17 (THE MESSAGE), *HOLY BIBLE*

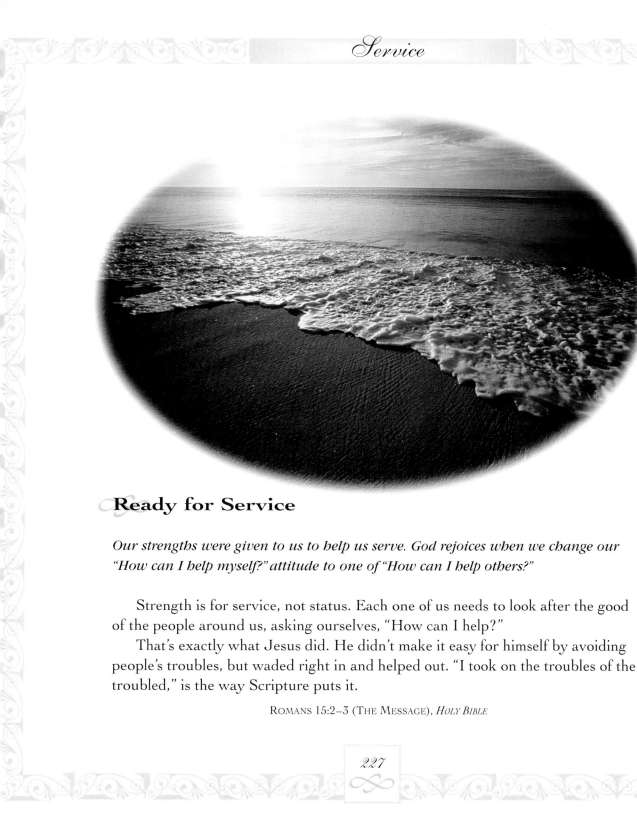

## Ready for Service

*Our strengths were given to us to help us serve. God rejoices when we change our "How can I help myself?" attitude to one of "How can I help others?"*

Strength is for service, not status. Each one of us needs to look after the good of the people around us, asking ourselves, "How can I help?"

That's exactly what Jesus did. He didn't make it easy for himself by avoiding people's troubles, but waded right in and helped out. "I took on the troubles of the troubled," is the way Scripture puts it.

ROMANS 15:2–3 (THE MESSAGE), *HOLY BIBLE*

# Desire Usefulness

*The search for pleasure, wealth, and fame often leads to frustration. It seems the more we get, the more we want. To be useful is a goal that brings rewards far beyond earthly pleasures.*

There are really only four great practical ends for which men and women can work in this world, — Pleasure, Wealth, Fame, and Usefulness. We owe it to ourselves to consider them carefully, and to make up our minds which of them is to be our chief object in life. . . . the one end that is really worth working for, — usefulness. To desire and strive to be of some service to the world, to aim at doing something which shall really increase the happiness and welfare and virtue of mankind — this is a choice which is possible for all of us; and surely it is a good haven to sail for. . . .

To have this for the chief aim in life ennobles and dignifies all that it touches. Wealth that comes as the reward of usefulness can be accepted with honour; and, consecrated to further usefulness, it becomes royal. Fame that comes from noble service, the gratitude of men, be they few or many, to one who has done them good, is true glory; and the influence

that it brings is as near to godlike power as anything that man can attain. But whether these temporal rewards are bestowed upon us or not, the real desire of the soul is satisfied just in being useful. The pleasant word that a man can hear at the close of the days, whispered in secret to his soul, is, "Well done, good and faithful servant!"

HENRY VAN DYKE,
*COUNSELS BY THE WAY* (1897)

*Anyone wanting to be the greatest must be the least—the servant of all.*

JESUS SPEAKING IN MARK 9:35 (TLB), *HOLY BIBLE*

## Things Servants Say

*The mark of a servant is willingness. We need to have an attitude of submitting to God's agenda rather than clinging to our own.*

"What shall I do. . . ?" Moses speaking.
—Exodus 17:4 (Amplified)

"Speak, Lord, for Your servant is listening."
Samuel speaking.—1 Samuel 3:10 (Amplified)

"Here am I. Send me!" Isaiah speaking.
—Isaiah 6:8 (NASB)

"Behold the maidservant of the Lord! Let it be to me according to your word." Mary speaking.—Luke 1:38 (NKJV)

"Not my will, but Thine be done." Jesus speaking.—Luke 22:42 (NASB)

"Lord, what do You want me to do?" Paul speaking.—Acts 9:6 (KJV)

## Receiving Service From Others

*Those of us who consider ourselves the Lord's servants sometimes have a hard time receiving from others. Although Jesus said, "It's more blessed to give than receive," this statement also says, "it is blessed to receive."*

While I was out for a couple hours,
my houseguests cleaned the house.
Instead of feeling grateful,
I felt hurt.
I know they were trying to help,
but I felt they were communicating,
"You are an inefficient housekeeper,
so we have to help you."
Why is it that I served them
the whole time they were here,
but when they tried to do a service
for me I couldn't handle it?
Didn't Jesus have the apostles wash
one another's feet and even his feet?
I only want to wash other people's feet.
Lord, please humble me enough
to let them wash mine.

## Love for God

*Love for God is the best motive for serving.*

If we are devoted to the cause of humanity, we shall soon be crushed and broken-hearted... but if our motive is love to God, no ingratitude can hinder us from serving our fellow men.

OSWALD CHAMBERS, *MY UTMOST FOR HIS HIGHEST* (1935)

## Let Your Light Shine Through Serving

You are the light of the world. A city set on a hill cannot be hid. Nor do men light a lamp and put it under a peck-measure but on a lamp stand, and it gives light to all in the house. Let your light so shine before men that they may see your moral excellence and praiseworthy, noble and good deeds, and recognize and honor and praise and glorify your Father Who is in heaven.

MATTHEW 5:14–16 (AMPLIFIED), *HOLY BIBLE*

# Serving God and Man

*What a mystery that when we serve our fellow man, it's as if we are doing the service for God.*

One of the principal rules of religion is to lose no occasion of serving God. And since he is invisible to our eyes, we are to serve him in our neighbor, which he receives as if done to himself in person, standing visibly before us.

JOHN WESLEY

## Jesus Explains Service to Others

*If we serve man, we serve God. If we serve the "least," we serve Jesus, because He came to earth to become one of the least.*

"'. . . for I was hungry and you gave Me food; I was thirsty and you gave Me drink; I was a stranger and you took Me in;

'I was naked and you clothed Me; I was sick and you visited Me; I was in prison and you came to Me.'

"Then the righteous will answer Him, saying, 'Lord when did we see You hungry and feed You, or thirsty and give You drink?

'When did we see You a stranger and take You in, or naked and clothe You?

'Or when did we see You sick, or in prison and come to You?'

"And the King will answer and say to them, 'Assuredly, I say to you, inasmuch as you did it to one of the least of these My brethren, you did it to Me.'"

MATTHEW 25:35–40 (NKJV), *HOLY BIBLE*

## Serving With a Purpose

*Work can be drudgery when we see it as just a job. Every area of work, no matter how insignificant it may seem, is an opportunity to faithfully serve God and man.*

For our God never considers our work as merely a way to earn a living—so much an hour, so much a year. He has given each of us the gift of life with a specific purpose in view. To Him work is a sacrament, even what we consider unimportant, mundane work. When done "as unto the Lord," it can have eternal significance.

CATHERINE MARSHALL,
*MEETING GOD AT EVERY TURN* (1981)

## A Full Life

*Those with the fullest and most fulfilling lives are those who are busy serving others.*

### Life

Life is a gift to be used every day,
Not to be smothered and hidden away;
It isn't a thing to be stored in a chest
Where you gather your keepsakes and treasure your best;
It isn't a joy to be sipped now and then
And promptly put back in a dark place again.

Life is a gift that the humblest may boast of
And one that the humblest may well make the most of.
Get out and live it each hour of the day,
Wear it and use it as much as you may;
Don't keep it in niches and corners and grooves,
You'll find that in service its beauty improves.

EDGAR A. GUEST, *A HEAP O' LIVIN'* (1916)

233

*The wonder of serving is when we meet the needs of others, forgetting about our own, and yet somehow in the process our needs are met.*

## Love for Those Who Serve

At night, Florence toured the wards with her lamp, making sure that everyone was comfortable . . . "What a comfort it was to see her pass," a soldier wrote home. "She would speak to one, and nod and smile to as many more, but she could not do it to all, you know. We lay there by hundreds, but we could kiss her shadow as it fell, and lay our heads on the pillow again, content."

PHILIPPA STEWART, *FLORENCE NIGHTINGALE* (1973)

*Serving God because you are God's friend puts a permanent end to duty.*

EUGENIA PRICE, *WHAT REALLY MATTERS* (1983)

## Serving the Dying

*Many people have found comfort through hospice care—both the terminally ill patients and their loved ones. Even the nurses, doctors, and volunteers who provide hospice care often find their own lives changed in the process.*

A friend who didn't drive asked if I could take her to the Hospice volunteer–training classes she was attending. My first reaction was to think of the discomfort I felt around dying people, even though I'd been a nurse years before—their suffering unnerved me. But I decided to take the classes with her, just to see what it was all about. Soon I discovered there were ways to ease my discomfort around dying people, but even more importantly, there were ways I could help ease their suffering. The main thing I saw in the volunteers and workers who helped us in the training was that they cared so much about people—I wanted to care that much, too.

At first it seemed painfully difficult to go into a stranger's room at the Hospice house where I've volunteered for the past 1½ years. I would plead to God: "Show me what to do and say!" And He has.

I've learned many things from serving as a Hospice volunteer. I've learned about dying with dignity and releasing one's suffering to God. I've learned how to be a better listener. I've learned how important it is to "seize the day," and even the moment—there are times I would say to myself, "I'll stop in and see her next time," and the next time wouldn't come because she had died. I've learned that even the little things matter—like a smile, a hug, holding someone's hand, reading from the Bible, or pushing a patient outside in a wheelchair.

I've learned about the power of prayer. One time a patient said, "I can't handle this anymore." I knew she believed in God, so I asked, "Do you want me to pray for you?" She said yes, so I did—out loud. God gave her peace and strength to make it over that hurdle.

I've learned that dying time can be a beautiful time, despite the suffering and uncertainty involved. I've learned how to mourn with those who mourn. I've learned about dealing with my own grief and loss and how to let go of self-pity, so I can cherish the act of living my life.

Serving with Hospice has given me an education no textbook could provide. And it has changed me—for the better.

A HOSPICE VOLUNTEER

## Serving in the Struggle for Freedom

*Martin Luther King had a dream that people of all races could be lifted from oppression. He dedicated his life to the service of the black community in order to fulfill that dream.*

What if he had died, he asked the audience, when he was stabbed in 1958 in Harlem? He would have missed the greatest experience of his life in the freedom struggle of the black people. There were difficult days ahead, he said, days of confusion and doubt to live through. He was not discouraged by this, on the contrary. "It really doesn't matter with me now. Because I've been to the mountaintop.... I've looked over and I've seen the Promised Land." Then he gave the people whom he had served so well his final promise, and his prophesy. "I may not get there with you," he said, "but I want you to know tonight, that we as a people will get to the Promised Land. So I'm happy tonight. I'm not worried about anything. I'm not fearing any man."

LILLIE PATTERSON, *MARTIN LUTHER KING, JR. AND THE FREEDOM MOVEMENT* (1989)

## On Being a Humble Servant

*Too many times we want to be known for the service we perform. But a humble servant is not concerned with praise or reward.*

Being a servant means serving without being thanked or recognized. It often entails giving and going unnoticed, being tired and not rested, sorrowful and not comforted. Servanthood by its very nature implies working behind the scenes, and it always demands quiet reliability on the part of the servant.

CHARLES SLAGLE, *FROM THE FATHER'S HEART* (1989)

*Whatever your task, work heartily, as serving the Lord and not men, knowing that from the Lord you will receive the inheritance as your reward; you are serving the Lord Christ.*

COLOSSIANS 3:23–24 (RSV), *HOLY BIBLE*

# One Group of Faithful Servants

*Teaching can be a thankless job with low pay and public criticism. It is a teacher's servant heart that can keep her going. Parents need to thank their children's teachers for their service.*

Some of the greatest servants
I know are teachers.
They don't get paid much
but they give much.
So many go the extra mile
to encourage my child.
To say, "You can do it—
I know you can."
They see beyond
the outer shell
to what's inside,
and they minister
to the heart
while trying to
teach the brain
to think.

They endure the criticism
of parents
and administration
and the press
and professional critics.
And still they serve on.
Rarely does a student say,
"Thank you for being
such a great teacher."
Often, we don't even think
of it until years later,
when we realize the impact
a teacher has made on our lives.
And so I thank you, teachers,
one and all
for being such faithful servants.

*All the service that weighs an ounce in the sight of God is that which is prompted by love.*

BILLY SUNDAY, *THE REAL BILLY SUNDAY* (1914)

# A Grateful Servant

*A dedicated servant is grateful to all those who have served him, including the Lord. He sees that he is passing on to others what he has received.*

As we drove home, I thought about how blessed I've been. I've received many honors and awards and much attention since accepting the Crystal Apple from President Reagan, but I realized that no award was greater than knowing Jesus Christ.

Not only had Jesus given me Himself, but He also had blessed me with a beautiful wife and children. Jesus had shown me love through common people—people who had molded and shaped my dreams, even when they didn't know they were teaching me.

GUY DOUD, 1986 TEACHER OF THE YEAR, *MOLDER OF DREAMS* (1990)

# Seeing Beyond the Dirt

*Seeing beyond the "dirt" to the beauty and goodness of those we serve is essential. We can do it if we look at them through the eyes of the Lord. This is seen in the following example, which the author based on her mother's experience teaching poor Appalachian children.*

"So please don't think I'm heroic. I've had just as much trouble adjusting to all of this as any of you would have. In fact, at first I almost gave up and went back home. It was a struggle to see underneath the rags and smells, the human beings—some with fine minds, some with great spirits, lovable, proud, sensitive—and begin to care about them, really care.

"It's like—well, like garden vegetables. If you threw out your turnips because they came out of the ground with dirt clinging to them, you'd never discover the goodness there."

CATHERINE MARSHALL, *CHRISTY* (1967)

## Serving With Words

*Some people have the ability to write words that lift the heart and soothe the soul.*
*Let's thank God for those who serve us in this way.*

I forget spoken words too easily,
and so I have appreciated
those who have served me
by sending notes
of encouragement
at just the right moment,
like the times I've battled
to maintain my faith,
and friends write to tell
of their own struggles
and God's faithfulness.
There was the time
I started to regret
not getting a teaching degree.
A friend wrote a note to say,
"Thank you for teaching me so much,"
reminding me a degree wasn't
necessary to teach others.
I remember the times
I've felt wounded by grief,
and notes that said, "I care"
or "I'm praying for you"
lifted my spirits.
I reread the notes that say,
"You are a wonderful friend"
when I'm feeling like a horrible person.
It's amazing that a few words
arranged in the proper order
can bring such relief
to an aching heart.
I will always cherish those
who serve me with their words.

## Serving Discreetly

*It's difficult to serve a fellow human being without letting other people know about it.*
*But God calls us to frequently engage in "secret service."*

Take care! Don't do your good deeds publicly, to be admired, for then you will lose your reward from your Father in heaven . . . But when you do a kindness to someone, do it secretly—don't tell your left hand what your right hand is doing. And your Father who knows all secrets will reward you.

Matthew 6:1, 3 (TLB), *Holy Bible*

## Service and Hard Work

*We tend to prefer indulgence to hard work, and we prefer hard work that is rewarded and praised.*
*But true servants work hard even when no one but God notices.*

I have been asked many times how I have succeeded in this thing or in that thing. In almost every case I have replied that it has required constant, hard, conscientious work. I consider that there is no permanent success possible without hard and severe effort, coupled with the highest and most praiseworthy aims. Luck, as I have experienced it, is only another name for hard work. Almost any individual can succeed in legitimate enterprise that he sets his heart upon, if he is willing to pay the price, but the price, in most cases, is being willing to toil when others are resting, being willing to work when others are sleeping, being willing to put forth the severest effort when there is no one to see or applaud. It is comparatively easy to find people who are willing to work when the world is looking on and ready to give applause, but very hard to find those who are willing to work in the corner or at midnight, when there is no watchful eye or anyone to give applause.

Booker T. Washington, *The Story of My Life and Work* (1901)

## *All service ranks the same with God.*

ROBERT BROWNING

## A Servant Reflects

*Billy Graham has served the Lord faithfully for decades, since he began preaching in 1938. Yet he sees where he could have done better—a sign of a truly humble servant.*

Although I have much to be grateful for as I look back over my life, I also have many regrets. I have failed many times, and I would do many things differently.

For one thing, I would speak less and study more, and I would spend more time with my family. When I look back over the schedule I kept thirty or forty years ago, I am staggered by all the things we did and the engagements we kept. Sometimes we flitted from one part of the country to another, even from one continent to another, in the course of only a few days. Were all those engagements necessary? Was I as discerning as I might have been about which ones to take and which to turn down? I doubt it. Every day I was absent from my family is gone forever.

BILLY GRAHAM, *JUST AS I AM* (1997)

*Serve the LORD with gladness . . .*

PSALM 100:2 (NASB), *HOLY BIBLE*

## Rewards of Serving

*There's a fulfilling joy that comes from serving other people rather than putting our own desires first.*

Rosalynn and I enjoy vacations, and we could go to Hawaii or on a Caribbean cruise every summer for about the same amount it costs us to travel to one of the Habitat building sites. But when I look back on the last twelve years or so, I see that some of my most memorable and gratifying experiences were when I joined other volunteers and worked to exhaustion building a house alongside the family who would live there.

JIMMY CARTER, *LIVING FAITH* (1996)

# Benefits From Service

*If we look to service for the benefits it will bring us, we may be disappointed. Yet, if we forget about the benefits and gladly serve others, good things happen to us. We are helped in so many ways by those we serve.*

*"He that watereth shall be watered also himself."* —*Proverbs 11:25.*

We are here taught the great lessons, that to get, we must give; that to accumulate, we must scatter; that to make ourselves happy, we must make others happy; and that in order to become spiritually vigorous, we must seek the spiritual good of others. In watering others, we are ourselves watered. How? Our efforts to be useful *bring out our powers for usefulness*. We have latent talents and dormant faculties, which are brought to light by exercise. Our strength for labor is hidden even from ourselves, until we venture forth to fight the Lord's battles, or to climb the mountains of difficulty. We do not know what tender sympathies we possess, until we try to dry the widow's tears, and sooth the orphan's grief. We often find, in attempting to teach others, that we *gain instruction for ourselves*. Oh, what gracious lessons some of us have learned at sick beds! We went to teach the Scriptures; we came away blushing that we knew so little of them. In our converse with poor saints, we are taught the way of God more perfectly for ourselves, and get a deeper insight into divine truth. So that watering others *makes us humble*. We discover how much grace there is where we had not looked for it, and how much the poor saint may outstrip us in knowledge. Our own *comfort is always increased* by our working for others. We endeavor to cheer them, and the consolation gladdens our own heart. Like the two men in the snow: one chafed the other's limbs to keep him from dying, and in so doing kept his own blood in circulation, and saved his own life.

CHARLES SPURGEON (1834–1892), *MORNING BY MORNING*

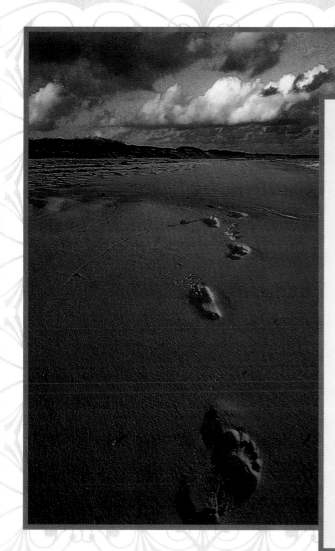

# Perseverance

There are many events in our lives over which we have no control. However, we do have a choice either to endure trying times and press on or to give up. The secret of survival, whether or not we question God's presence or His ability to help us, is remembering that our hope is in the fairness, goodness, and justice of God. When we put our trust in the character of a God who cannot fail us, we will remain faithful. Our trust and faithfulness produce the endurance that sees us through the "tough stuff" we all face in this life.

## Don't Quit

*For several decades, this famous poem has hung on refrigerator doors in homes across America and has been mailed to discouraged college students by their mothers.*

When things go wrong, as they sometimes will,
When the road you're trudging seems all up hill,
When the funds are low and the debts are high,
And you want to smile, but you have to sigh,
When care is pressing you down a bit,
Rest, if you must—but don't you quit.

Life is queer with its twists and turns,
As every one of us sometimes learns,
And many a failure turns about
When he might have won had he stuck it out;
Don't give up, though the pace seems slow—
You might succeed with another blow.

Often the goal is nearer than
It seems to a faint and faltering man,
Often the struggler has given up
When he might have captured the victor's cup.
And he learned too late, when the night slipped down,
How close he was to the golden crown.

Success is failure turned inside out—
The silver tint of the clouds of doubt—
And you never can tell how close you are,
It may be near when it seems afar;
So stick to the fight when you're hardest hit—
It's when things seem worst that you must not quit.

CLINTON HOWELL

## The Broken String

*We often face tasks that seem to have insurmountable odds. But if we make the most of whatever we have, the results are guaranteed to be beautiful.*

Paganini, the world-famed violinist, was once playing before an audience when, in the midst of his brilliant performance, a string snapped. He played on, only to have a second fail him. With but two strings he continued his rendition. Then a third broke. With but one string at his command the master-player, unfaltering and undismayed, proceeded to the end with such brilliance and skill that his audience burst into a frenzy of applause. Paganini was but a man; our master-player is God. We may seem to ourselves to be of little use, dull and unresponsive, gifted with but a single string, yet if the instrument of our lives be wholly given up to Him, He will use it to bring forth heavenly glory under the power and skill of his touch.

NORMAN B. HARRISON, *HIS VERY OWN* (1930)

*Great works are performed not by strength but by perseverance.*

SAMUEL JOHNSON (1709–1784)

## Provoke One Another

*There's an often misunderstood verse in the Bible: "And let us consider one another to provoke unto love and to good works" (Hebrews 10:24, KJV).*

In this context, the above verse means that we are to arouse, incite, hearten. What a wonderful character quality: to be able to awaken and inspire others to live righteously and godly in this present world.

We don't often think about how much failure is simply due to the lack of incentive or courage or loss of spirit. When we "lose heart" in our projects, there is no longer any vision to propel us toward our goals. This is when we can become cheerleaders to our struggling friends. This is how we hearten and provoke others to good works.

It was the bricklayer, singing to the merry ring of his trowel, and continuing his tedious job on the wall, who aroused Carlyle from the stupor of his despondency and provoked him to rewrite the second volume of his *History of the French Revolution.*

## Sometimes It Means Beginning Again

*There are times when we are forced to do a laborious task—and then do it all over again. But if we follow it through to the end, the results can be better than we ever expected. The following story about author Thomas Carlyle (1795-1881) is an excellent example.*

We all have dreams of what we want to achieve during our lifetime. But few "endure to the end" to see their God-given dreams become realities. To achieve our dreams we must first set a long-range goal and objective. For many this is difficult because of vague ideas about what they might want to do "sometime." Without specific goals, nothing significant can happen.

After we have set our objective, we must think about the specific steps we can take to reach this goal. As we take each step, we are making a commitment to press on. The only thing that helps us at this stage is perseverance. Perseverance makes it possible for us to believe that we can accomplish what we've set out to.

Thomas Carlyle had finished writing his tremendous manuscript, *History of the French Revolution* (1837). He gave it to his neighbor, John Stuart Mill, to read. Several days later, Mill came to Carlyle's home pale and nervous to report to Carlyle that his maid had used the manuscript to start a fire!

Carlyle was in a frenzy for days. Two years of labor lost. He could never muster the energy to write again. A task that large was overwhelming the first time. The thought of having to write the whole thing over was almost paralyzing.

One day, as Carlyle was walking the streets, he saw a stonemason building a long, high wall. He stood watching for a long time before he was suddenly impressed with the fact that the wall was being built one brick at a time! He took inspiration from that experience and decided, "I'll just write one page today, and then one page tomorrow. One page at a time, that's all I'll think about."

He started small and slow. The task was tedious, but he stayed with it and went on to finish the work. The end result was better than the first time!

Don't let bad memories or unfortunate incidents move in and dominate you. You won't get very far by looking in the rear-view mirror—you must look ahead! Perseverance enables you to live in such a way that you can *make* good things happen.

## The Spur to Untiring Service

*When we remember that we are working for the rewards of heaven and not for the praise of people, we are able to press on and persevere in the tasks ahead of us.*

How much this teaching is needed in a day of superficial and man-made methods to maintain good works in the face of flagging energies.... How many dear people of God are fainting in their service because men are slow to approve or slightly applaud. Stung to inaction by the sense of ingratitude! We all need to turn often to these Scriptures to nerve us to renewed service. Men require a sense of reward, somehow, somewhere. We have it, fully assured, from Him and in Him. Beyond all that He may give us will be Himself. Anticipating the sight of His face then, we need to see Him now, as the antidote to faintness and weariness, the sufficient spur to untiring service.

NORMAN B. HARRISON, *HIS VERY OWN* (1930)

*Keep up the good work and don't get discouraged, for you will be rewarded.*

2 CHRONICLES 15:7 (TLB), *HOLY BIBLE*

*Have courage for the great sorrows of life and patience for the small ones; and when you have laboriously accomplished your daily task, go to sleep in peace. God is awake.*

VICTOR HUGO (1802–1885)

## Gratitude for Work

Thank God every morning when you get up that you have something to do which must be done, whether you like it or not. Being forced to work, and forced to do your best, will breed in you temperance and self-control, diligence and strength of will, cheerfulness and content, and a hundred virtues which the idle never know.

CHARLES KINGSLEY (1819–1875)

*And let us not be weary in well doing: for in due season we shall reap, if we faint not.*

GALATIANS 6:9 (KJV), *HOLY BIBLE*

## Keep on Working

Though I walk in the midst of trouble, thou dost preserve my life; thou dost stretch out thy hand against the wrath of my enemies, and thy right hand delivers me. The Lord will fulfil his purpose for me; thy steadfast love, O Lord, endures for ever. Do not forsake the work of thy hands.

PSALM 138:7–8 (RSV), *HOLY BIBLE*

*Because the Lord God helps me, I will not be dismayed; therefore, I have set my face like flint to do his will, and I know that I will triumph.*

ISAIAH 50:7 (TLB), *HOLY BIBLE*

## When You Feel Defeated

*Too many of us let the little things in life defeat us. But many outstanding figures in history have had to overcome obstacles before they became successful— perhaps that is part of what made them so great.*

There is a man who once lived in America who inspires all of us, yet this man knew the meaning of defeat. His mother died when he was a child. As a young man, he ran for the legislature of his state, but he was defeated.

He entered business, but a worthless partner put him into bankruptcy. He fell passionately in love with a girl, but she died.

He served one term in Congress, but was defeated for re-election. He tried for an appointment to the United States Land Office, but failed to get it. He tried to be a lyceum lecturer, but he failed in that also.

He ran for the United States Senate, but was defeated. He ran for vice-president of the United States, but was defeated.

His name was Abraham Lincoln.

CHARLES L. ALLEN, *WHEN YOU GRADUATE* (1972)

## Try, Try Again

*Many parents have quoted this favorite old poem to their children. The lesson may be simple, but it's an important one to learn!*

'Tis a lesson you should heed,
    Try, try again;
If at first you don't succeed,
    Try, try again;
Then your courage should appear,
For, if you will persevere,
You will conquer, never fear;
    Try, try again.

Once or twice though you should fail,
    Try, try again;
If you would at last prevail,
    Try, try again;
If we strive, 'tis no disgrace
Though we do not win the race;
What should you do in this case?
    Try, try again.

Time will bring you your reward,
    Try, try again.
All that other folks can do,
Why, with patience, should not you?
Only keep this rule in view;
    Try, try again.

W. E. HICKSON (1803–1870)

## Let God Make Something Beautiful of Your Life

*Our situations and circumstances may look pretty bleak, but when we take time to look at the accomplishments of others who have persevered, we can take heart and have courage.*

Tired, depressed, discouraged? Take heart. God is not done with you yet. We used to sing a song in youth revivals:

Got any rivers you think are uncrossable?
Got any mountains you can't tunnel through?
God specializes in things thought impossible;
And he can do what no other power can do.

Then comes the challenge: "Let go and let God have His wonderful way...."

The greatest men and women seem to have suffered the most. Remember the Apostle Paul's celebrated "thorn in the flesh"? We are not told the ailment. It could have been failing eyesight, epilepsy, piercing headaches, hearing impairment, or something else. He "besought the Lord" three times that it might depart. How did God answer? "He said unto me," wrote Paul, "'My grace is sufficient for you: for my strength is made perfect in weakness.'"

How did the great apostle respond? "Most gladly therefore will I rather glory in my infirmities, that the power of Christ may rest upon me" (2 Corinthians

12:7–9). He "let go and let God" have his wonderful way.

Your life is only over if you think it is. You can learn to "glory" in your infirmities and build a bridge out of them to find God's purpose for the rest of your life.

Think about. . . .

Bill Wilson, a "hopeless alcoholic," founding Alcoholics Anonymous, which has brought sobriety to millions.

John Milton doing his greatest literary work after he became blind at forty-four.

Corrie ten Boom becoming a world inspiration with her books and films. She had been released from a Nazi concentration camp in her fifties, after she had lost her entire family.

Ludwig von Beethoven creating his greatest symphonies after he started going deaf. Vowed the music master: "I will seize life by the throat."

But you need not draw inspiration from just the famous. Draw from the example of LaRue Moss who was told by her father when she left for college, "Honey, if you're going to reach out for the stars, first you have to put out your hand."

LaRue aspired to be an educator. First she fell in love. Six weeks after the wedding she broke her back in a car wreck. It was three years before she could walk again.

She almost died in childbirth and was bedridden for a year.

Finally she went back and completed her bachelor's degree in elementary education — sixteen years after her father had first taken her to the bus station to leave for college. She attended school while operating a lawn mowing business to help support her family.

She enrolled for a master's while continuing to mow lawns. She was studying for her doctorate at Vanderbilt University in Nashville when a hit-and-run driver struck her down. Despite chest injuries and a bruised heart, she managed to stay in graduate school.

A dull backache continued and intensified. The doctor said she might be paralyzed within twenty-four hours if she didn't have surgery. Leaving her incomplete dissertation, she was whisked into the operating room.

She awoke in a sunlit yellow room to see the beaming faces of her family. "I thought I had died and gone to heaven," she said. Then, looking at her sister she asked, "Hey, did you bring my dissertation back from the waiting room?"

Sixteen months later this brave woman who kept "reaching for the stars" received her doctorate in education.

Take God. Take hold. Move out. Reach up. Reach for the stars. Let God make something beautiful out of your life.

JAMES C. HEFLEY, *LIFE CHANGES* (1984)

"Come to Me, all you who labor and are heavy-laden and over-burdened, and I will cause you to rest — I will ease and relieve and refresh your souls. Take My yoke upon you, and learn of Me; for I am gentle (meek) and humble (lowly) in heart, and you will find rest — relief, ease and refreshment and recreation and blessed quiet — for your souls. For My yoke is wholesome (useful, good) — not harsh, hard, sharp or pressing, but comfortable, gracious and pleasant; and My burden is light and easy to be borne."

MATTHEW 11:28–30 (AMPLIFIED), *HOLY BIBLE*

## Blessed Assurance

*This popular hymn may best be remembered as the theme song that George Beverly Shea led the choir and congregation in singing at every Billy Graham evangelistic crusade.*

Blessed assurance, Jesus is mine!
Oh what a foretaste of glory divine!
Heir of salvation, purchase of God,
Born of His Spirit, washed in His blood.

Perfect submission, perfect delight!
Visions of rapture now burst on my sight;
Angels descending bring from above
Echoes of mercy, whispers of love.

Perfect submission—all is at rest,
I in my Savior am happy and blest;
Watching and waiting, looking above,
Filled with His goodness, lost in His love.

Chorus:
This is my story, this is my song,
Praising my Savior all the day long;
This is my story, this is my song,
Praising my Savior all the day long.

FANNY J. CROSBY (1820–1915)

*Commit everything you do to the Lord. Trust him to help you do it and he will.*

PSALM 37:5 (TLB), *HOLY BIBLE*

# Stand By Your Work

*The following excerpt is from the Letter to Teachers that C. E. Leslie wrote in the front of his often-used music textbook. In it, he reminds us that teaching and music are two of life's greatest pursuits, and that no matter what our profession is, we should always perform with our best efforts, creativity, and the highest enthusiasm.*

Dear Teacher,

Your success greatly depends on your own efforts; you must be intensely interested in your profession.

Do not devote all your time to the study of music, but to the study of development; of how best to teach your pupils to comprehend it. The successful teacher is the one who can, in the most simple way, and in the shortest space of time, teach his pupils to understand the subject under consideration.

Do not confine yourself to text books; be original; use the black-board, make your exercises short and to the point. Do not dwell too long on one subject; keep your pupils interested. After you have taught them to read music, have them frequently study silent singing. Silent singing is *thought getting*. Oral singing is the *giving of the thought* from the printed page, and we must have the thought before we can give it to others.

Teachers, again let me urge you to be honest and faithful in the profession you have chosen. Stand by the work twelve months in the year. Separation means loss of power. You may be doing only rudimental work, but if honestly and well done, it will meet with God's approval.

Music is one of God's greatest gifts to man. Electric wires, railroads and steamships make the whole world as one city; but the vibrations of music produce the only electric current that binds earth to heaven. When you are singing, "O for a closer walk with God!" it may be rudimental work, but it is the only power you can call upon for relief, or that will satisfy your weary heart. When you sing, "I know that my Redeemer Liveth," it may be the echo as it comes back to us from that heavenly shore: "Peace, peace, peace to thy weary soul!" Rudimental work is the foundation upon which all of our lives are builded. Be not ashamed of your position. When a great General falls in battle his life and heroic deeds are heralded to all the world upon the pages of history. The private soldier who shouldered his musket, bade his loved ones good-by, and went to his death in defense of his country, fills perhaps an unknown grave; but in God's book of memory his name is registered, and the angels have written opposite, the word Hero. It is not the position that tells, but the earnest and conscientious discharge of the duties belonging to it. Be faithful in the work entrusted to your care.

Teacher, if I can help you on to success, let me know it. I am your friend, use me as such.

Yours, very truly, C. E. Leslie

C. E. LESLIE, *LESLIE'S CROWN OF SONG*, JANUARY 15, 1890

*God, you're leading me.*
*With confidence I face my day.*
*Every duty and interruption*
*are appointments*
*you've sent my way.*

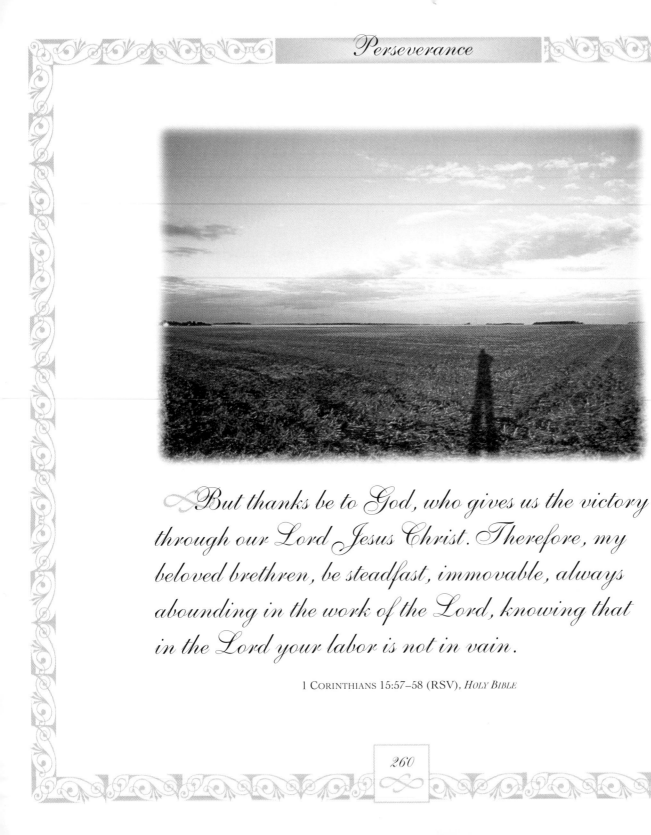

*But thanks be to God, who gives us the victory through our Lord Jesus Christ. Therefore, my beloved brethren, be steadfast, immovable, always abounding in the work of the Lord, knowing that in the Lord your labor is not in vain.*

1 CORINTHIANS 15:57–58 (RSV), *HOLY BIBLE*

# O God, Our Help in Ages Past

*This old hymn of the church is taken from the words of Psalm 90.*

O God, our help in ages past,
    Our hope for years to come,
Our shelter from the stormy blast,
    And our eternal home!

Under the shadow of Thy throne,
    Still may we dwell secure;
Sufficient is Thine arm alone,
    And our defense is sure.

Before the hills in order stood,
    Or earth received her frame,
From everlasting Thou art God,
    To endless years the same.

A thousand ages, in Thy sight,
    Are like an evening gone;
Short as the watch that ends the night,
    Before the rising sun.

O God, our help in ages past,
    Our hope for years to come,
Be Thou our guide while life shall last,
    And our eternal home.

ISAAC WATTS (1674–1748)

*He that overcometh shall inherit all things; and I will be his God, and he shall be my son.*

REVELATION 21:7 (KJV), *HOLY BIBLE*

# A Psalm of Life

*This poem reminds us that as we journey through life we can leave "footprints on
the sands of time" for those who follow behind us.*

Tell me not, in mournful numbers,
    Life is but an empty dream!
For the soul is dead that slumbers,
    And things are not what they seem.

Life is real! Life is earnest!
    And the grave is not its goal;
Dust thou art, to dust returnest,
    Was not spoken of the soul.

Not enjoyment, and not sorrow,
    Is our destined end or way;
But to act, that each to-morrow
    Finds us farther than to-day.

Art is long, and Time is fleeting,
    And our hearts, though stout and brave,
Still, like muffled drums, are beating
    Funeral marches to the grave.

In the world's broad field of battle,
    In the bivouac of Life,
Be not like dumb, driven cattle!
    Be a hero in the strife!

Trust no Future, howe'er pleasant!
    Let the dead Past bury its dead!
Act—act in the living Present!
    Heart within, and God o'erhead!

Lives of great men all remind us,
    We can make our lives sublime,
And departing, leave behind us
    Footprints on the sands of time;

Footprints, that perhaps another,
    Sailing o'er life's solemn main,
A forlorn and shipwrecked brother,
    Seeing, shall take heart again.

Let us, then, be up and doing,
    With a heart for any fate;
Still achieving, still pursuing,
    Learn to labour and to wait.

HENRY WADSWORTH LONGFELLOW (1807–1882)

## Perseverance Means More Than Endurance

*God will not delay a minute longer than necessary to bring us the direction, answers, and relief we seek and pray for.*

Perseverance means more than endurance—more than simply holding on until the end. A saint's life is in the hands of God like a bow and arrow in the hands of an archer. God is aiming at something the saint cannot see, but our Lord continues to stretch and strain, and every once in a while the saint says, "I can't take any more." Yet God pays no attention; He goes on stretching until His purpose is in sight, and then He lets the arrow fly. Entrust yourself to God's hands. Is there something in your life for which you need perseverance right now? Maintain your intimate relationship with Jesus Christ through perseverance of faith.

OSWALD CHAMBERS, *MY UTMOST FOR HIS HIGHEST* (1992)

## Perseverance Is Courage Stretched Out

*Tim Hansel's near-fatal accident taught him much about the importance of perseverance. The accident, which happened in 1974, is detailed in his book* You Gotta Keep Dancin'.

I was with a friend, doing snow-, ice-, and rock-climbing on a splendid day. We had concluded a wonderful climb, and were almost back to the bottom. All we had to do was cross the snow bridge over one crevasse, which, as you know, is a huge opening in the ice where a glacier pulls apart. This one happened to be about five stories deep.

We were tired yet exuberant from our exhilarating climb. Neither of us

had noticed that the surface of the snow over the crevasse had changed, causing the ordinarily firm footing to be slippery. Snow began balling up under my crampons (spikes attached to the bottom of a hiker's boots) until I suddenly slipped. In a flash, I slid down to the edge, flipped over upside down, and fell toward the bottom where I landed on the back of my neck.

It could have been worse. The ice pick around my wrist could have skewered me. And the large boulder at the bottom could have broken my neck. But it could have been a lot better, too. If I hadn't flipped over, my legs would have hit first instead of my upper body. If there had been anything between me and the bottom to break the fall, my impact wouldn't have been so devastating.

But when I came to, I surprised both

my friend and myself by actually getting up, climbing out of the crevasse with him and hiking back to the base camp. Everything seemed okay as we returned home, until the shock wore off. And that's when the splitting, aching, agony of pain hit.

From that moment, my life has never been the same. After rounds and rounds of doctors and x-rays, I was told that I had fractured vertebrae and several crushed discs, and that there were bone fragments in my neck. I was lucky I wasn't a quadraplegic, they all said. I was indeed fortunate just to be alive.

But later, I was finally told that the pain would be permanent; it would be intense and chronic. That was the way it would be. So, as the struggles continued, I had to decide what power the pain would have over my life. I still had a choice, I realized. The choice wasn't as easy as people imagine. And it continues to be a daily, sometimes hourly, choice to make. The lessons about perseverance come daily and hourly, too.

Perseverance is courage stretched out. One of the biblical words for it suggests that it is courage under pressure, under strenuous conditions. Since the writing of *You Gotta Keep Dancin'*, about my struggle to choose joy over pain, I've had people ask me if I am joyous all the time. Somehow many readers came to believe that in my choosing to persevere in as joyful a way as I can, my pain somehow vanished. Or if not that, I evidently had such strength of will that I overcame the pain to the extent that I now live in continual joy.

It's just not so. . . .

Perseverance is not an easy quality, yet it's not a quality for a select few. Most of the time, it involves an amount of courage that we would never believe we could have. It's a unique combination of patience plus endurance. It's what makes life worthwhile in spite of adversity. And quite often, it involves a quality of letting go and letting God keep us at it, funneling his power through us to keep us from quitting. I must confess that there are days I want to crawl into the corner and never come out.

However, I know full well that I don't have a corner on the pain market. I simply share these things to help us realize more fully that we all face tough times, emotionally and physically, and as we feel discouraged, we all think about giving up. At one time or another, giving up is exactly what we're all tempted to do in any undertaking or any crisis that stretches us, because such tough situations open us up to risk and failure.

TIM HANSEL, *HOLY SWEAT* (1987)

*And let us not get tired of doing what is right, for after a while we will reap a harvest of blessing if we don't get discouraged and give up.*

GALATIANS 6:9 (TLB), *HOLY BIBLE*

*Perseverance is possible as long as we remain convinced that God is at work—changing people, changing our circumstances, and changing us.*

*Better is the end of a thing than the beginning thereof: and the patient in spirit is better than the proud in spirit.*

ECCLESIASTES 7:8 (KJV), *HOLY BIBLE*

## Persevere in Obedience

*"What is faith? It is the confident assurance that something we want is going to happen. It is the certainty that what we hope for is waiting for us, even though we cannot see it up ahead"* (Hebrews 11:1, TLB).

A problem
and a promise—
God has not left us
unarmed.
He has made a way of escape;
He will not have us
harmed.
Persevere in obedience—
He may be testing
your faith.
But He will lead you
victoriously
to arrive at
your
promised place.

## Trusting God's Promises

*God may throw us a few curves in life—we may feel hassled, troubled, anxious, or uncomfortable, and not understand why our circumstances don't fit our desires. But if we trust in the wisdom of His plan, God will provide for all our needs.*

It was November 1978. My husband, Bob, bounced through the front door of our Boise, Idaho, home calling, "Hi Honey! How was your day?"

An ominous feeling crept over me. Was it the tone of his voice? An unusual lilt to his usually fast-paced walk? Something was definitely different.

"Oh, it was OK. How about yours?" I replied guardedly.

"Super. Today I got a promotion and we're moving back to Helena."

My mouth dropped open. I managed a muted "Oh! When?" My world suddenly seemed to be crashing in around me. We'd moved six times in the past fifteen years, to Texas, California, Montana, Alaska, Washington, D.C., and Boise. But to go back to Montana...it had been my least favorite place.

Why had God regarded my husband's prayers more than my own? I asked Him, "God, do you know what you're doing? Why do we need to be uprooted now?"

God gets my attention best when I'm in His Word, so I flipped open my Bible. My eyes landed on Joshua 22:5: *"Love the Lord and follow his plan for your lives. Cling to him and serve him enthusiastically."* Then I saw: *"But follow the Lord your God just as you have until now....for the Lord your God fights for you, just as he has promised. So be very careful to keep on loving him"* (Joshua 23:8, 10, 11, TLB).

"Okay, God. I don't understand it but... how will we ever be able to sell our home or get the money to buy a new one? The market is so tight right now, and no one buys and sells houses at Christmastime. It'll never work."

Next I read, *"Look! I'm living here in a cedar-paneled home.... Carry out your plan in every detail, for it is the will of the Lord....And I have been with you everywhere you've gone"* (1 Chronicles 17:1, 2, 8, TLB).

Our house sold the first week it was on the market. We made it through sorting, packing, farewell parties, and moving—though we didn't yet have a new house to move into. Helena became a test in perseverance. I dreaded the daily trudging through snowdrifts in 20-degree weather to house-hunt. My fear of getting stuck in a snowbank became a reality several times. I wanted to go back inside, dive under the covers, and spend the day watching TV. But living in a motel was so depressing. We had to find a house *soon*!

I looked at ten houses a day for ten days, and nothing seemed right for us. I'd definitely not found the new cedar-paneled home I had expected since God spoke to me through his Word. "God, am I wrong? Was I reading more into that Scripture than what you intended? Where do you want us to live? Where shall I look today? I don't even know which way to turn anymore. Help me please," I cried out as I stared at my coffee cup in the coffee shop.

My dejection turned to despair when the realtor arrived to show me today's "picks." He had just one home to show that might meet our needs. When we arrived at the new house, he discovered the lock box had been removed from the door, so we couldn't even get in! I remained in the car wondering about the futility of this trip, then turned to look at beautiful Mt. Helena rising a block to the north. This was definitely the location that we would prefer, *if only* there was something available.

Then I saw a home being built across the street. "God, that's it! I know it! That's the cedar home you promised me!" Excitedly, I yelled for the realtor. "Can we go across the street and see the one under construction?"

His negative answer, "It's not one of my listings," didn't dampen my spirits.

"Then please, sir, take me back to the hotel so I can get my car. I must see that house. It's 'For Sale by Builder.'"

It took me less than fifteen minutes to return to the dream home on the hill. My feet flew up the steps, "Is anyone here?"

A young man approached. "How can I help you?"

"Could you tell me what kind of wood is on the outside of this house? And on the fireplace wall?" My first questions no doubt sounded a little strange to the small cluster of men I'd just noticed working in the corner.

"Why, it's all cedar paneling," the builder answered.

"Is the house still for sale?" I asked breathlessly.

"Yes. Although that group of realtors just came to list it," he replied motioning to the front window.

"Oh, please hold it for me. I know it's the one that God has chosen for us, but I must run and call my husband to come from work."

My husband's reply was, "If it's the house God has for us, then go ahead and buy it!"

I managed to restrain myself for thirty minutes until he arrived from his office. But there was never a doubt. God had done more than I could ask or think. Why had I ever doubted that I could trust him with every detail of my life? As I wrote out our deposit check, I breathed a silent prayer, "God, thank you for once again showing how greatly you care for every detail of our lives."

# Smile—God Loves You!

*Trials are a fact of life. The question is: What are you going to do about them?*

Your temptations and trials point up the weak spots in your character and show the areas in your defense that need immediate attention. You need buttressing and shoring up, and some of it is going to hurt.

It is only when the trials do come that some of us get know Him at all, and begin to perceive what He might be trying to do with us.

But He does care: "*...and I concentrate myself to meet their need for growth in truth and holiness...*" He cares beyond anything your finite mind can get ahold of.

ETHEL BARRETT, *IT ONLY HURTS WHEN I LAUGH* (1973)

## Stand Fast!

*It is easy to have self-pity and resent the painful trials and heartaches that come into our lives. But God always works for our greater good.*

As difficult as it may be for you to believe this today, the Master knows what He's doing. Your Savior knows your breaking point. The bruising and crushing and melting process is designed to reshape you, *not to ruin you*. Your value is increasing the longer He lingers over you.

A.W. Tozer agrees:

*It is doubtful whether God can bless a man greatly until He has hurt him deeply.*

Aching friend—stand fast. Like David when calamity caved in, strengthen yourself in the Lord your God (1 Samuel 30:6). God's hand is in your heartache. Yes, it is!

If you weren't important, do you think He would take this long and work this hard on your life? Those whom God uses most effectively have been hammered, filed, and tempered in the furnace of trials and heartache.

CHARLES R. SWINDOLL, *COME BEFORE WINTER* (1985)

## God Will Sustain Me

*God, Himself, has said, "I will not in any way fail you, nor give you up, nor leave you without support. I will not, I will not, I will not, in any degree leave you helpless, nor forsake nor let you down" (Hebrews 13:5, Amplified).*

People may fail me, friends seem to forsake me, and my family may act like they either don't care or don't understand. It is easy to become discouraged and tempting to give up when I look around at my circumstances.

But I will persevere—claiming the promise that God will not abandon me or fail me (Joshua 1:5). With the apostle of old I will confidently say, "The Lord is my Helper, I will not be seized with alarm—I will not fear or dread or be terrified. What can man do to me?" (Hebrews 13:6, Amplified).

## Praying for Strength

O God . . . Help me to link my littleness to Thy greatness, my faintheartedness to Thy loving aggression, my holding back to Thy ongoingness, my fear to Thy faith—then nothing can stop me. Amen.

E. Stanley Jones, *Abundant Living* (1942)

# Wisdom

The Bible urges us to "Acquire wisdom! Acquire understanding!" (Proverbs 4:5). We are instructed to have two goals: Wisdom—knowing and doing right—and common sense. Wisdom is the ability to meet each situation with discernment and good judgment, whether in dealing with others, making choices, or dispensing justice. Wisdom involves using the knowledge we have to take the proper course of action—if we know and don't act, it is the same as not knowing at all. When we let Christ become the source of our wisdom, He will guide us in making wise decisions and acting on them.

*Wisdom is more precious than rubies; nothing you desire can compare with her.* PROVERBS 3:15 (NLT), *HOLY BIBLE*

## The Beginning of Wisdom

*When we really want to acquire wisdom, we must start by getting to know God better.*

Teach the wise, and they will be wiser. Teach the righteous, and they will learn more. Fear of the Lord is the beginning of wisdom. Knowledge of the Holy One results in understanding. Wisdom will multiply your days and add years to your life. If you become wise, you will be the one to benefit. If you scorn wisdom, you will be the one to suffer.

PROVERBS 9:9–12 (NLT), *HOLY BIBLE*

## To Be Counted Wise

*To be known as a wise person, it's important to use your knowledge well and not flaunt it.*

Do you want to be counted wise, to build a reputation for wisdom?
Here's what you do: Live well, live wisely, live humbly.
It's the way you live, not the way you talk, that counts.
Mean-spirited ambition isn't wisdom.
Boasting that you are wise isn't wisdom.
Twisting the truth to make yourselves sound wise isn't wisdom.
It's the furthest thing from wisdom—it's animal cunning, devilish conniving.
Whenever you're trying to look better than others or get the better of others,
things fall apart and everyone ends up at the others' throats.

Real wisdom, God's wisdom, begins with a holy life and is
characterized by getting along with others.
It is gentle and reasonable, overflowing with mercy and blessings,
not hot one day and cold the next, not two-faced.
You can develop a healthy, robust community that lives right with God
and enjoy its results *only* if you do the hard work of getting along with
each other, treating each other with dignity and honor.

JAMES 3 (THE MESSAGE), *HOLY BIBLE*

## Wisdom and Understanding

And the Spirit of the Lord will rest on him—the Spirit of wisdom and understanding, the Spirit of counsel and might, the Spirit of knowledge and the fear of the Lord. He will delight in obeying the Lord. He will never judge by appearance, false evidence, or hearsay. He will defend the poor and the exploited. He will rule against the wicked and destroy them with the breath of his mouth. He will be clothed with fairness and truth.

ISAIAH 11:2–5 (NLT), *HOLY BIBLE*

## The Wise Man's Glory

*God's highest priority is that we get to know Him and live a life that reflects His love and justice.*

Thus saith the Lord, Let not the wise man glory in his wisdom, neither let the mighty man glory in his might, let not the rich man glory in his riches: But let him that glorieth glory in this, that he understandeth and knoweth me, that I am the Lord which exercise lovingkindness, judgment, and righteousness, in the earth: for in these things I delight, saith the Lord.

JEREMIAH 9:23–24 (KJV), *HOLY BIBLE*

*When did you last pause to recognize God's wisdom in the timing of events in your life? Have you thanked Him?*

## Making a Difference

*We all want to do something effective in this world while we are here. The key is being faithful to what God lays on our heart.*

There is a universal desire among people today: to make a difference. The biggest roadblock in finding "where" we can be most effective is not knowing our purpose and our calling. When we make a decision to seek God's wisdom it will mean: (1) Getting to know God better so we can apply His wisdom in all our decisions; (2) Waiting patiently for God to open and close doors as He engineers our circumstances; (3) Doing what is closest at hand that we know is God's will. For example: God's concern for the poor is evident in nearly every book of the Bible. Central to following God is seeing that the poor and oppressed around us are treated fairly. When we cultivate a compassionate spirit, we mirror God's love and concern for a needy world.

God has given each of us a purpose for living, and when we are serious about wanting to know it and faithful to obey what He shows us, we can trust Him to guide us into that place of His perfect will.

## Wisdom Speaks

Listen as wisdom calls out! Hear as understanding raises her voice! She stands on the hilltop and at the crossroads. At the entrance to the city, at the city gates, she cried aloud, "I call to you, to all of you! I am raising my voice to all people. How naïve you are! Let me give you common sense. O foolish ones, let me give you understanding. Listen to me! For I have excellent things to tell you. Everything I say is right, for I speak the truth and hate every kind of deception. My advice is wholesome and good. There is nothing crooked or twisted in it. My words are plain to anyone with understanding, clear to those who want to learn.

"Choose my instruction rather than silver, and knowledge over pure gold. For wisdom is far more valuable than rubies. Nothing you desire can be compared with it.

"I, Wisdom, live together with good judgment. I know where to discover knowledge and discernment. All who fear the Lord will hate evil. That is why I hate pride, arrogance, corruption, and perverted speech. Good advice and success belong to me. Insight and strength are mine. Because of me, kings reign, and rulers make just laws.

Rulers lead with my help, and nobles make righteous judgments.

"I love all who love me. Those who search for me will surely find me. Unending riches, honor, wealth, and justice are mine to distribute. My gifts are better than the purest gold, my wages better than sterling silver! I walk in righteousness, in paths of justice. Those who love me inherit wealth, for I fill their treasuries.

"The Lord formed me from the beginning, before he created anything else. I was appointed in ages past, at the very first, before the earth began. I was born before the oceans were created, before the springs bubbled forth their waters. Before the mountains and the hills were formed, I was born—before he had made the earth and fields and the first handfuls of soil.

"I was there when he established the heavens, when he drew the horizon on the oceans. I was there when he set the clouds above, when he established the deep fountains of the earth. I was there when he set the limits of the seas, so they would not spread beyond their boundaries. And when he marked off the earth's foundations, I was the architect at his side. I was his constant delight, rejoicing always in his presence.

And how happy I was with what he created—his wide world and all the human family!

"And so, my children, listen to me, for happy are all who follow my ways. Listen to my counsel and be wise. Don't ignore it.

"Happy are those who listen to me, watching for me daily at my gates, waiting for me outside my home! For whoever finds me finds life and wins approval from the Lord. But those who miss me have injured themselves. All who hate me love death."

PROVERBS 8 (NLT), *HOLY BIBLE*

## If You Need Wisdom, Ask God

If any of you need wisdom, you should ask God, and it will be given to you. God is generous and won't correct you for asking. But when you ask for something, you must have faith and not doubt. Anyone who doubts is like an ocean wave tossed around in a storm. If you are that kind of person, you can't make up your mind, and you surely can't be trusted. So don't expect the Lord to give you anything at all.

JAMES 1:5–8 (THE PROMISE), *HOLY BIBLE*

# Wisdom:
## The Sought-After Virtue

*Having knowledge is not the same as having wisdom. The true test of wisdom is knowing how and when to act, according to God's will.*

Rare and scarce,
precious and priceless,
inestimable and invaluable.

These are just a few words which describe that desirable attribute, that much sought after virtue which men call wisdom. English poet Samuel Taylor Coleridge once wrote, "Common sense in an uncommon degree is what the world calls wisdom." Webster puts it this way, "Wisdom is the quality of being wise; it is knowledge with capacity to use it; it is the perception of the best ends and the best means."

Wisdom is that virtue which enables a man to make decisions as God would make them. Putting it another way, a wise man is one who solves his problems in the same manner as God would solve them.... One commentator wrote, "Through knowledge man has learned to travel faster than sound but shows his lack of wisdom by going faster in the wrong direction." Charles Haddon Spurgeon had it right when he said, "Wisdom is the right use of knowledge. To know is not to be wise. Many men know a great deal and are all the greater fools for it. There is no fool so great a fool as a knowing fool. But to know how to use knowledge is to have wisdom."...

True wisdom is available to man through prayer. One day David found himself involved in a battle with the Philistines in the Valley of Rephaim. God instructed David to encircle the enemy and come in from behind at the point where the mulberry trees were located. He was told that when he heard a stirring in those trees, he was to begin the attack. This he did, carrying out God's counsel to the letter. As a result he won an overwhelming victory (2 Samuel 5:22–25).

HAROLD L. FICKETT, JR., *JAMES* (1972)

*Wisdom is a tree of life to those who embrace her; happy are those who hold her tightly.* PROVERBS 3:18 (NLT), HOLY BIBLE

*True spiritual maturity, the product of time spent in the Word and continuous walking in the Spirit, manifests itself when Christ's will and your will are synonymous.*

TIM LaHAYE, *HOW TO WIN OVER DEPRESSION* (1974)

## To Know God — Study Him

I wish you could truly begin the study of God. This must be our delight throughout eternity. It is the happiest and most helpful study that can possibly engage our thoughts. Why cannot we know God without study? Because all knowledge is thus acquired. To learn a thing without study is to forget it. To learn and not use, is also to forget. Life is unhappy to many because they know so little of God. Those who know Him best are most anxious to know more of Him.

DAVID C. COOK, *THE SECRET OF HAPPY HOME-LIFE* (1898)

*Christianity makes one educated, cultured, and moral, but these things do not make a Christian.*

AUTHOR UNKNOWN

*From a wise man comes careful and persuasive speech.*

PROVERBS 16:23 (TLB), *HOLY BIBLE*

## The Eternal God Is Thy Refuge

*H. O. Van Gilder, a past president of Western Baptist College, told this story on several occasions during chapel services in the 1960s. It reminds us that wisdom includes not just knowing, but also trusting and doing.*

Recently, we heard of a building project where workmen were working throughout the night. One of the workmen, alone on the edge of a wall several stories high, suddenly lost his balance and fell. Grasping wildly, he was able to grip the edge of the wall with his fingers.

Desperately, he clung to the narrow ledge, hoping soon to be discovered. In the dark shadows below the level of the wall, his shouts and cries for help were to no avail. The noise and chatter of the riveting machines, the puffing of the hoisting engines, and the myriad other sounds in the huge construction project muffled all his calls.

Soon he felt his arms grow numb. Even with intense effort to hold his fingers rigid, they began to relax against the heavy strain. Frantically, he tried to pray, but there was no miracle.

At last, his fingers slipped from the wall. With a last retching sob of terror, he fell—about three inches to a scaffold that had been there in the darkness all the time!

How like a lot of Christians! Thinking their salvation depends on their own endurance, and conscious of their weakness, they are fearful, anxious, and unhappy most of the time. Yet, "underneath are the everlasting arms" (Deuteronomy 33:27, KJV). All the while a faithful, loving, and all-powerful God is waiting to rescue us.

# U. S. Presidents on Biblical Wisdom

*Throughout the ages, men who've held the United States' highest office have gathered wisdom from the highest authority of all.*

George Washington (1732–1799), the first President of the United States once said, "I now make my earnest prayer that God would be most graciously pleased to dispose us all to do justice, to love mercy, and to demean ourselves with that charity, humility, and pacific temper of mind which were the characteristics of the divine Author of our blessed religion."

President Ulysses S. Grant (1822–1885) said: "Hold fast to the Bible as the sheet anchor of your liberties. Write its precepts in your hearts, and practice them in your lives. To the influence of this Book are we indebted for all the progress made in true civilization, and to this we must look as our guide in the future" (1876, *The Sunday School Times*).

President William McKinley, our 25th President, said: "The more profoundly we study this wonderful book, and the more closely we observe its divine precepts, the better citizens we will become and the higher will be our destiny as a nation."

Theodore Roosevelt (1858–1919), the United States' 26th President, is quoted as saying, "Almost every man who has by his life-work added to the sum of human achievement of which the race is proud, of which our people are proud, almost every such man has based his life-work largely upon the teachings of the Bible."

President Calvin Coolidge (1872–1933), when presented a Bible while in office said, "In this little book will be found the solution to all the problems of the world."

Woodrow Wilson (1856–1924), the 28th President, said: "A man has deprived himself of the best there is in the world who has deprived himself of this [a knowledge of the Bible]. . . . There are a good many problems before the American people today, and before me as President, but I expect to find the solution of those problems just in the proportion that I am faithful in the study of the Word of God."

President Herbert Hoover (1874–1964) said, "There is no other book so varied as the Bible, nor one so full of concentrated wisdom. Whether it be of law, business, morals, or that vision which leads the imagination in the creation of constructive enterprise for the happiness of mankind, he who seeks for guidance in any of these things may look inside its covers and find illumination. The study of this Book in your Bible classes is a post-graduate course in the richest library of human experience. As a nation we are indebted to the Book of books for our national ideas and representative institutions. Their preservation rests in adhering to its principles."

And President Jimmy Carter said, "We believe that the first time we're born, as children, it's human life given to us; and when we accept Jesus as our Savior, it's a new life. That's what 'born again' means." (March 16, 1976)

## Acquire Wisdom

Get wisdom, get understanding;
do not forget my words or swerve from them.
Do not forsake wisdom, and she will protect you;
love her, and she will watch over you.
Wisdom is supreme; therefore get wisdom.
Though it cost all you have, get understanding.

PROVERBS 4:5–7 (NIV), *HOLY BIBLE*

# Wise Words and Important Truths

*It is important that a wise person passes on their wisdom—not only in words, but in deeds.*

Because the Teacher was wise, he taught the people everything he knew. He collected proverbs and classified them. Indeed, the Teacher taught the plain truth, and he did so in an interesting way.

A wise teacher's words spur students to action and emphasize important truths. The collected sayings of the wise are like guidance from a shepherd.

But, my child, be warned: There is no end of opinions ready to be expressed. Studying them can go on forever and become very exhausting!

Here is my final conclusion: Fear God and obey his commands, for this is the duty of every person. God will judge us for everything we do, including every secret thing, whether good or bad.

ECCLESIASTES 12:9–13 (NLT), *HOLY BIBLE*

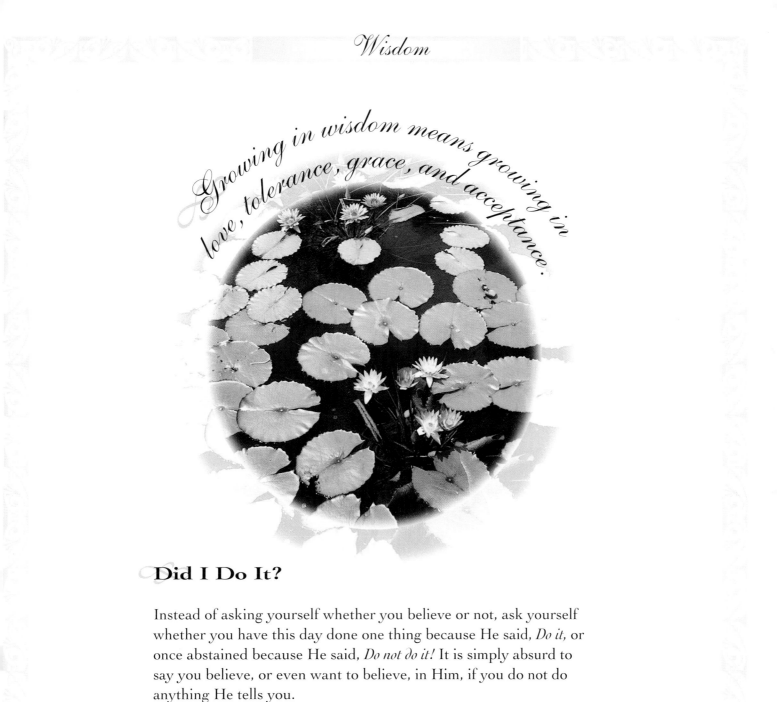

*Growing in wisdom means growing in love, tolerance, grace, and acceptance.*

## Did I Do It?

Instead of asking yourself whether you believe or not, ask yourself whether you have this day done one thing because He said, *Do it*, or once abstained because He said, *Do not do it!* It is simply absurd to say you believe, or even want to believe, in Him, if you do not do anything He tells you.

GEORGE MACDONALD

287

# Following God's Guidance

*Whenever we are uncertain as to our course, we can rely on God, in His wisdom, to shut doors against us—every door but the right one.*

God guides His people through His Word, by circumstances, and by the peace in our Spirit. When we are "willing" to follow what we sense that God is telling us to do, we are never left wondering for long as to which way we should go.

When we cooperate with God as He engineers the circumstances of our lives, there is no limit to what He can do. God opens and closes the doors before us at His will. When we don't understand what He is doing, we do well to remember that we are not fulfilled by the plans we create, but rather by following God's plan for us.

*And those who are wise—the people of God—shall shine as brightly as the sun's brilliance, and those who turn many to righteousness will glitter like stars forever.*

DANIEL 12:3 (TLB), *HOLY BIBLE*

# On Prudence in Action

*Millions of people through the ages have read the words of Thomas à Kempis and endeavored to put his words into practice in their daily lives.*

We should not believe every word and suggestion, but should carefully and unhurriedly consider all things in accordance with the will of God. For such is the weakness of human nature, alas, that evil is often more readily believed and spoken of another than good. But perfect men do not easily believe every tale that is told them, for they know that man's nature is prone to evil, and his words to deception.

It is wise not to be over hasty in action, nor to cling stubbornly to our own opinions. It is wise also not to believe all that we hear, nor to hasten to report to others what we hear or believe. Take counsel of a wise and conscientious man, and seek to be guided by one who is better than yourself, rather than to follow your own opinions. A good life makes a man wise towards God, and gives him experience in many things. The more humble and obedient to God a man is, the more wise and at peace he will be in all that he does.

THOMAS À KEMPIS, *THE IMITATION OF CHRIST;*
TRANSLATED BY LEO SHERLEY-PRICE

# The Power of Affirmation

*God has given each person a storehouse of wisdom and creativity. But to fully tap into our potential, we have to believe in ourselves—and it helps to know that others believe in us, too. In fact, it can make all the difference.*

We all know how very much it means to be believed in. There was a study done by a group of researchers from Harvard. They would go to elementary school teachers at the beginning of the school year and tell them that they had designed a test which could prove most helpful to them. The results would correctly predict which students were going to grow intellectually during the coming school year. Someone called it "The Harvard Test of Intellectual Spurts" because he said it told which students were going to "spurt" that year. The educators promised it would pick out the right students and it was very, very accurate.

Given permission to give the test, they administered, unbe-

knownst to the teacher, an old, obsolete I.Q. test. When the students had finished the test, the papers were collected and the researchers threw them in the wastebasket. Then they picked five names at random from the roll book and sat down with the teachers and said, "Now these are the students in your class who are going to have a very good year. Watch these kids. One of them is Rachel Smith," they informed the teacher.

"Rachel Smith?" the teacher replied incredulously, "She wouldn't 'spurt' if you shot her from a cannon. I have had two of her brothers and each one of the Smiths is dumber than the last." But the educators maintained that the test hardly ever was wrong in its findings and that Rachel's progress in the ensuing year could be readily observed.

You can imagine what happened that semester, can't you? Yes, you can. Rachel never had a chance to be her same old self. Under a barrage of "Rachel, would you write this on the board this morning," "Rachel will lead the line to the lunch room today,"

"Is that a new dress, Rachel? It sure is pretty," "Thank you, Rachel, that was very good," Rachel 'spurted' all over the place. And so did every name they put on that list.

According to the Apostle Paul, every one of our names belongs on a list like that. We are all "God's chosen people, holy and dearly loved." I think one of my all-time favorite quotes is from a little boy in elementary school who said, "My teacher thought I was smarter than I wuz. So I wuz!" And all of us need to be in a group that believes we are smarter and better and more gifted than we have ever dared to think we were. For this is one of the ways that each of us will begin to hear the calling voice of God.

We need to see that we are to be giving life even as we are receiving it, that we are to be nurturing even as we are being nurtured, that we are to be healing even as we are being healed.

One of the things that the hand on our shoulder is saying to each of us is a deep, affirmative, "I believe in you." And we should be saying to the one whose shoulder we are touching, "I believe in who you are, and what you can become, because of the gifts that God has put within you."

BOB BENSON, *SEE YOU AT THE HOUSE* (1986)

## A Prayer for Wisdom

Dear Lord, help me to build on a firm foundation by relying on your wisdom, diligently seeking your direction in all I do, learning to walk in your paths of kindness, peace, and justice to my fellowman. In Jesus' name, Amen.

*Don't refuse to accept
criticism; get all the help you can.*

PROVERBS 23:12 (TLB), *HOLY BIBLE*

*Wisdom comes through a constant process of growth!
Don't depend on inspiration or luck—plan to prevail
by good planning and steady work.*

PROVERBS 2:10, *LIFE APPLICATION BIBLE NOTES* (TLB)

*The intelligent man is always open to new ideas.*
*In fact, he looks for them.*

Proverbs 18:15 (TLB), *Holy Bible*

# What Would Jesus Do?

*In 1935, the book* In His Steps *was the most popular book—with the exception of the Bible— that had ever been written. Over 30,000,000 copies were sold in all corners of the world and in all languages. The theme of the book is as relevant today as ever.*

Henry Maxwell's face was wet with tears. If an audible voice from heaven had sanctioned their pledge to follow the Master's steps, not one person present could have felt more certain of the divine blessing. And so the most serious movement ever started in the First Church of Raymond was begun.

"We all understand," said he, speaking very quietly, "what we have undertaken to do. We pledge ourselves to do everything in our daily lives after asking the question, 'What would Jesus do?' regardless of what may be the result to us. Some time I shall be able to tell you what a marvelous change has come over my life within a week's time. I cannot now. But the experience I have been through since last Sunday has left me so dissatisfied with my previous definition of Christian discipleship that I have been compelled to take this action. I did not dare begin it alone. I know that I am being led by the hand of divine love in all this. The same divine impulse must have led you also.

"Do we understand fully what we have undertaken?"

CHARLES SHELDON (1857–1946), *IN HIS STEPS*

# In His Own Words...
# About *In His Steps*

*A fundamental part of wisdom is having access to information. Here, Charles Sheldon explains how, through a happy "accident," In His Steps became the second most widely distributed book of its time.*

From the foreword:

THE STORY "In His Steps" was written in 1896, and it was read a chapter at a time to my young people, Sunday evenings in the Central Congregational Church, Topeka, Kansas. While it was being read it was being published in the *Chicago Advance*, a religious weekly, as a serial. The publisher did not know the conditions of the copyright law, and he filed only one copy of the *Advance* each week with the department, instead of two, which the law required. On that account the copyright was defective, and the story was thrown into the "public domain" when the Advance Company put it out in a ten cent paper edition. Owing to the fact that no one had any legal ownership in the book, sixteen different publishers in America and fifty in Europe and Australia put out the book in various editions from an English penny to eight shillings. Mr. Bowden, the London publisher, sold over 3,000,000 copies of the penny edition on the streets of London.

The book has been translated into twenty-one languages, including a Russian publication which has been banned by the Soviet. A Turkish translation in Arabic is permitted circulation by the government and is being read all over Turkey.

The story has been made into the drama form and is being used by groups of young church people and by college students. And while conditions have changed in the years since the story was written, the principle of human conduct remains the same. I do not need to say that I am very thankful that owing to the defective copyright, the book has had a larger reading on account of the great number of publishers. I find readers in every part of the world where I go. And I am informed by the *Publishers' Weekly* that the book has had more circulation than any other book except the Bible. If that is true, no one is more grateful than I am, as it confirms the faith I have always held that no subject is more interesting and vital to the human race than religion.

CHARLES M. SHELDON (1935)

## Seeking Wisdom?

*We are sometimes faced with choices that are scary, risky, and untried. But we can make wise decisions if we rely on God's spiritual guidance.*

Are you on the verge of a decision? Is the Lord loosening your tent pegs today, suggesting it's time for you to take a drastic leap of faith? Are you counting on Him to direct your steps through a future that offers no tangible map? Great! But before you jump, be sure of four things:

— Be sure it's the Lord who is speaking.

— Be sure the decision doesn't contradict Scripture.

— Be sure your motive is unselfish and pure.

— Be sure the "leap" won't injure others or your testimony.

Sometimes it helps to remember what God calls us during our short stint on Planet Earth: strangers and pilgrims. People on the move, living in tents, free and unencumbered, loose and available, ready to roll, willing to break the mold—whenever and wherever He leads. Regardless.

CHARLES R. SWINDOLL, *COME BEFORE WINTER* (1985)

## I Know Not Why

*Our lives are filled with many questions that may never be answered, but that's okay if we let God lead and direct us. We may not understand why certain things happen or why we have to go through difficult situations. But the one thing we can know for sure is that God is always in charge.*

I know not why His hand is laid
    In chastening on my life,
Nor why it is my little world
    Is filled so full of strife.
I know not why, when faith looks up
    To seek release from pain,
That o'er my sky fresh clouds arise
    To drench my path with rain.
I know not why my prayer so long
    By Him has been denied,
Nor why, when other ships sail on,
    Mine should in port abide.
But I do know that God is love,
    That He my burden bears,
So tho' I do not understand,
    One thing I know . . . He cares!
I know the heights for which I yearn
    Are often reached through pain.
I know that sheaves must needs be threshed
    To yield their golden grain.
I know that though He may remove
    The friends on whom I lean,
'Tis that I thus may learn to love
    And trust the One unseen.
And when at last my race is run,
    And Heaven's joys I've known,
I will not care how rough the road
    That lead through Christ, to Home.
For whate'er my lot in life may be,
    One thing I know . . . He leadeth me!

AUTHOR UNKNOWN

## Reward of Mercy

*While we are all familiar with systems of punishment and reward, a wise person will know when to dispense justice and when to be merciful.*

I was raised in the strict tradition that if one did wrong one should be punished for it. That was called justice.

In 1921, as a young doctor, I took over the post of medical officer to a fever hospital in a bleak and isolated district of Northumberland. One winter evening, shortly after my arrival, a diphtheria case was admitted: a little boy of six so desperately choked with membrane that an immediate tracheotomy offered the only slender chance of saving him.

Painfully inexperienced, I had never attempted this simple but crucial operation. As I stood in the bare, lamp-lit ward and watched the old sister and the only nurse — a junior probationer — place the gasping child upon the table I felt myself trembling, cold and sick.

I began the operation: a nervous incision into that thin, congested throat. As I fumbled on, conscious of my own incompetence, a resolution to succeed, to save this suffocating child took possession of me. At last the stem of the trachea showed white

and shining under my sweat-dimmed eyes. I slit it and a rush of air filled the child's struggling chest. Again and again the tortured lungs expanded. As new strength flooded the exhausted little body, I could have cried aloud in relief. Quickly I slipped in the tracheotomy tube, completed the sutures, saw the child comfortable in his steam-tented bed. I went back to my own quarters in a glow of triumphant joy.

Four hours later, at two o'clock in the morning, I was roused by a frantic knocking at my door. It was the young nurse. White-faced, hysterical, she stammered: "Doctor, doctor, come quickly."

She had drowsed off by the child's cot and awakened to find that the tube had become blocked. Instead of following instructions and clearing the tube of membrane, a matter of nursing routine, she had lost her head and committed the unpardonable sin of bolting in panic. When I got to the ward the child was dead. Nothing we could do was of any avail.

The sense of loss, the needless, culpable waste of human life overwhelmed me. Worst of all was the thought of my precious case wrecked by the blundering negligence of a frightened nurse. My anger blazed at white heat. Of course her career was finished. I would send a report to the County Health Board, and she would be kicked out of the hospital, expelled from the nursing body to which she belonged.

That evening I dipped my pen in vitriol and wrote the indictment. I summoned her and read it to her in a voice burning with indignation.

She heard me in pitiful silence. She was a raw Welsh girl of about 19, thin and rather gawky, with a nervous tremor of her cheek. Anemic and undernourished, she was now half-fainting with shame and misery.

Her failure to make any sort of excuse—she might with some justification have pleaded that she was worn out with overwork—stung me into exclaiming: "Have you nothing to say?"

She shook her head wanly. Suddenly she stammered: "Give me another chance."

I was taken aback. The idea had never entered my head. My sole thought was to make her pay for what she had done. I stared at her, then dismissed her curtly. I signed and sealed my report.

All through that night I was strangely troubled. "Give me another chance." A queer echo kept drumming in my head, an echo which whispered that my justice, that all justice was no more than a primitive desire for revenge. Angrily I told myself not to be a fool.

Yet next morning I went to the letter rack and tore up my report.

That was 20 years ago. Today the nurse who erred so fatally is matron of the largest children's home in Wales. Her career has been a model of service and devotion. Only a week ago I received a photograph showing a middle-aged woman in matron's uniform, surrounded by children, in an air-raid shelter. She looks harassed and weary; but the childish eyes which gaze at her are filled with trust and love.

"Forgive us our trespasses as we forgive those that trespass against us." It's hard to practice that simple prayer. But, even in this life, it pays.

A. J. CRONIN, IN *READER'S DIGEST*, SEPTEMBER 1941

*A person can accumulate immense knowledge and still lack wisdom. Wisdom requires compassion, justice, humility, and spiritual discernment.*

## Seek Wisdom Seriously

We all know people who never find wisdom, because they don't seek it seriously. Wisdom comes easily only to those who pay attention to experienced people and to God. If the wisdom you need does not come easily to you, perhaps your attitude is the barrier.

PROVERBS 14:6, *LIFE APPLICATION BIBLE NOTES* (TLB)

## Hearing the Truth

A lot of poor advice is worth less than a little good advice. It is easy to get opinions from people who will tell us only what they think will please us, but such advice is not helpful. Instead we should look for those who will speak the truth, even when it hurts. Think about the people to whom you go for advice. What do you expect to hear from them?

PROVERBS 10:20, *LIFE APPLICATION BIBLE NOTES* (TLB)

*The world will judge our doctrines by our deeds.*

AUTHOR UNKNOWN

*Who among you is wise and understanding? Let him show by his good behavior his deeds in the gentleness of wisdom.*

JAMES 3:13 (NAS), *HOLY BIBLE*

## Live As Those Who Are Wise

So be careful how you live, not as fools but as those who are wise.
Make the most of every opportunity for doing good in these evil days.
Don't act thoughtlessly, but try to understand what the Lord wants you to do.

EPHESIANS 5:15–17 (NLT), *HOLY BIBLE*

## Priority Check

*Our lives are often bogged down by unimportant time-wasters. A wise person makes the best use of every moment.*

If we knew we had a week to live, our priorities would fall into place, not by degrees as we tidied up our lives, and not by making a checklist in order of importance and experimenting with it—but in one split second. There would be no time for specious reasoning and not a breath to waste. Absolutely everything that was not impor- tant would fall away as if it had never been.

ETHEL BARRETT,
*IT ONLY HURTS WHEN I LAUGH* (1973)

# Joy

When we think of joy, we often think of things that are new — a new day, a new baby, a new love, a new beginning, the promise of a new home with God in heaven. Rejoicing in these things originates with having joy in the God who makes all things new. Rather than relying on earthly pleasures to provide happiness, the Scriptures command that we rejoice in God and in each new day He brings. Joy is a celebration of the heart that goes beyond circumstances to the very foundation of joy — the knowledge that we are loved by God.

303

# Shout for Joy!

*When we experience true joy, we will naturally express it. As God pours joy into our lives, we can bring it back to Him.*

Shout for joy to the LORD, all the earth. Worship the LORD with gladness; come before him with joyful songs. Know that the LORD is God. It is he who made us, and we are his; we are his people, the sheep of his pasture. Enter his gates with thanksgiving and his courts with praise; give thanks to him and praise his name. For the LORD is good and his love endures forever; his faithfulness continues through all generations.

PSALM 100 (NIV), *HOLY BIBLE*

Rejoice in the Lord always; again I will say, rejoice!

PHILIPPIANS 4:4 (NASB), HOLY BIBLE

*Though now you do not see Him, yet believing,*
*you rejoice with joy inexpressible and full of glory.*

1 PETER 1:8 (NKJV), *HOLY BIBLE*

# Dance for Joy

*Cultures throughout the world have used dance to express joy. Dancing is done at feasts, at weddings, and at almost every other celebration. In fact, God's word commands us to dance as an expression of worship and joy.*

For all those who are afraid to dance for joy, here is a challenge. Go home and put on your favorite music that honors God. Listen to the words carefully or put on classical music, which speaks without words. Let the burdens and cares of life float away. Contemplate all God has done for you. Think about the loving family you have. Think of all the times God has saved them from harm when your arms of protection weren't long enough. Remember the times God rescued you from hopelessness and depression. Think of how so many sorrows have passed when it seemed they never could. Concentrate on the love of God—the wonder of His plan for mankind—the fact that the God of the universe wants a love relationship with us—with you. Think about the truth that if you were the only one on earth, Jesus would have laid down His life for you—

you count that much with Him. Think of what your heavenly home will be like. Think of the mansion and streets of gold that await you. Think of dancing on those streets as you go to meet your departed loved ones and see Jesus face to face. Let your feet and your body respond to the joy that is in you. Dare to dance as an expression of joy.

How can dancing be wrong when Scripture says, "You have turned for me my mourning into dancing" (Psalm 30:11, NKJV)? And what about the celebration when the prodigal son came home? Scripture says that the older son "heard music and dancing" as part of the celebration (Luke 15:25). There was the dancing in celebration after the Israelites had crossed the Red Sea: "Then Miriam, the prophetess, Aaron's sister, took a tambourine in her hand, and all the women followed her, with tambourines and dancing" (Exodus 15:20, NIV). And was it wrong when David "danced before the LORD with all his might . . . leaping and whirling before the LORD" (2 Samuel 2:14, 16)? Psalm 149:3 gives this instruction: "Praise Him with the timbrel and dance . . . " Ecclesiastes says there is "a time to mourn, and a time to dance . . . " (verse 4).

Every place in Scripture that refers to dancing has to do with rejoicing. It is one way to rejoice before God and in God. Certainly one can choose a dance that rejoices in vulgarity or sensuousness or worldliness, but does that mean we cannot choose to rejoice in the Lord through dancing? Dance before the Lord as David did. Let Him lead.

There is much to rejoice about. Let fear and inhibition depart. Go ahead—dance for joy.

*Weeping may endure for a night, but joy cometh in the morning.*

PSALM 30:5 (KJV), *HOLY BIBLE*

## Free to Show Joy

*It is wonderful to watch an uninhibited person express joy. We long to give our souls permission to rejoice so freely.*

My rosy-cheeked boy stood still, watching with wide-eyed fascination the gyrating dance of the Down syndrome girl as she scooped up leaves and showered herself with a twirling rain of autumn jubilation.

With each twist and hop she sang, deep, earthy grunts—a canticle of praise meant only for the One whose breath causes the leaves to tremble from the trees.

Hurry up. Let's go. Seat belts on? I start the car. In the rearview mirror I study her one more time through misty eyes. And then the tears come. Not tears of pity for her. The tears are for me. For I am too busy to dance in the autumn leaves and far too sophisticated to publicly shout praises to my Creator.

I am whole and intelligent and normal, and so I weep because I will never know the severe mercy that frees such a child and bids her come dance in the autumn leaves.

ROBIN JONES GUNN, "AUTUMN DANCE," IN
*MOTHERING BY HEART* (1996)

## When Laughter Fades

*Laughter is such a part of joy that when it fades in a loved one, our hearts can feel like they are about to break. The return of laughter brings renewed joy.*

One of the worst things about my ten-month-old's sickness, which the doctors called "failure to thrive" and which led to weeks in the hospital, was when she reached a point where she did not laugh. Before she got sick, she loved to repeatedly cover and un-cover her eyes and laugh heartily every time I said, "Peek-a-boo." Often I'd tickle her tummy and say, "Coochie, coochie coo," as she laughed gleefully. I tried these when she was in the hospital. It broke my heart that she would not, could not laugh or even smile.

I remember the day I wearily prayed, telling God how much I missed her laughter. Shortly after, I went up to her room, and for the first time in days, she played all the little games, and she laughed and laughed. It was like medicine to my soul. The next day, the laughter disappeared again, but it was enough to help me through the rest of her illness. She is a healthy teen now, and I still love to hear the sound of her laughter.

I wonder, Does God love to hear the sound of our laughter? Does it break His heart too when we are no longer able or willing to laugh for joy? Does it lift Him up when we resume our laughter? I believe the answer to these questions is "Yes. Yes. Yes."

# Sweet Sorrow

*It seems whatever brings us the greatest joy also brings sorrow. Every mother knows that. We would not feel such sorrow if we did not have such great love for our children.*

### The Sorrow Tugs

There's a lot of joy in the smiling world,
    there's plenty of morning sun,
And laughter and songs and dances, too
    whenever the day's work's done;
Full many an hour is a shining one, when
    viewed by itself apart,
But the golden threads in the warp of life are
    the sorrow tugs at your heart.

Oh, the fun is froth and it blows away, and
    many a joy's forgot,
And the pleasures come and the pleasures go,
    and memory holds them not;
But treasured ever you keep the pain that causes
    your tears to start,
For the sweetest hours are the ones that bring
    the sorrow tugs at your heart.

The lump in your throat and the little sigh when
    your baby trudged away
The very first time to the big red school—how
    long will the memory stay?
The fever days and the long black night you
    watched as she troubled, slept,
And the joy you felt when she smiled once
    more—how long will that all be kept?

The glad hours live in a feeble way, but the sad
    ones never die.
His first long trousers caused a pang and you
    saw them with a sigh.
And the big still house when the boy and girl,
    unto youth and beauty grown,
To college went; will you e'er forget that first
    grim hour alone?

It seems as you look back over things, that all
    that you treasure dear
Is somehow blent in a wondrous way with a
    heart pang and a tear.
Though many a day is a joyous one when
    viewed by itself apart,
The golden threads in the warp of life are the
    sorrow tugs at your heart.

EDGAR A. GUEST, *A HEAP O' LIVIN'* (1916)

## Trust Means Joy

*We can maintain our joy when we remember how faithful and unchanging God is. Focusing on Him brings renewed joy.*

The root of faith produces the flower of heart-joy. We may not at the first rejoice, but it comes in due time. We trust the Lord when we are sad, and in due season He so answers our confidence that our faith turns to fruition and we rejoice in the Lord. Doubt breeds distress, but trust means joy in the long run. . . .

Let us meditate upon the Lord's holy name, that we may trust Him the better and rejoice the more readily. He is in character holy, just, true, gracious, faithful and unchanging. Is not such a God to be trusted? He is allwise, almighty, and everywhere present; can we not cheerfully rely on Him? . . . They that know thy name will trust thee; and they that trust thee will rejoice in thee, O Lord.

CHARLES SPURGEON (1834–1892), *FAITH'S CHECKBOOK*

## The Lost Is Found

*There is great joy when lost things are found—lost lambs, lost coins, but especially lost people. Sometimes we lose our joy, like the older brother in the story of the prodigal son. The good news is that we can turn to God and find it again.*

"Suppose one of you had a hundred sheep and lost one. Wouldn't you leave the ninety-nine in the wilderness and go after the lost one until you found it? When found, you can be sure you would put it across your shoulders, rejoicing, and when you got home call in your friends and neighbors, saying, 'Celebrate with me! I've found my lost sheep!' Count on it—there's more joy in heaven over one sinner's rescued life than over ninety-nine good people in no need of rescue.

"Or imagine a woman who has ten coins and loses one. Won't she light a lamp and scour the house, looking in every nook and cranny until she finds it? And when she finds it you can be sure she'll call her friends and neighbors: 'Celebrate with me! I found my lost coin!' Count on it—that's the kind of party God's angels throw every time one lost soul turns to God."

Then he said, "There was once a man who had two sons. The younger said to his father, 'Father, I want right now what's coming to me.'

"So the father divided the property between them. It wasn't long before the younger son packed his bags and left for a distant country. There, undisciplined and dissipated, he wasted everything he had. After

he had gone through all his money, there was a bad famine all through that country and he began to hurt. He signed on with a citizen there who assigned him to his fields to slop the pigs. He was so hungry he would have eaten the corncobs in the pig slop, but no one would give him any.

"That brought him to his senses. He said, 'All those farmhands working for my father sit down to three meals a day, and here I am starving to death. I'm going back to my father. I'll say to him, "Father, I've sinned against

God, I've sinned before you; I don't deserve to be called your son. Take me on as a hired hand.'" He got right up and went home to his father.

"When he was still a long way off, his father saw him. His heart pounding, he ran out, embraced him, and kissed him. The son started his speech: 'Father, I've sinned against God, I've sinned before you; I don't deserve to be called your son ever again.'

"But the father wasn't listening. He was calling to the servants, 'Quick. Bring a clean set of clothes and dress him. Put the family ring on his finger and sandals on his feet. Then get a grain-fed heifer and roast it. We're going to feast! We're going to have a wonderful time! My son is here—given up for dead and now alive! Given up for lost and now found!' And they began to have a wonderful time.

"All this time the older son was out in the field. When the day's work was done he came in. As he approached the house, he heard the music and dancing. Calling over one of the houseboys, he asked what was going on. He told him, 'Your brother came home. Your father has ordered a feast—barbecued beef!—because he has him home safe and sound!'

"The older brother stalked off in an angry sulk and refused to join in. His father came out and tried to talk to him, but he wouldn't listen. The son said, 'Look how many years I've stayed here serving you, never giving you one moment of grief, but have you ever thrown a party for me and my friends? Then this son of yours who has thrown away your money on whores shows up and you go all out with a feast!'

"His father said, 'Son, you don't understand. You're with me all the time, and everything that is mine is yours—but this is a wonderful time, and we had to celebrate. This brother of yours was dead, and he's alive! He was lost, and he's found!'"

LUKE 15: 3–32 (THE MESSAGE), *HOLY BIBLE*

*"You're with me all the time, and everything that is mine is yours—but this is a wonderful time, and we had to celebrate. This brother of yours was dead, and he's alive! He was lost, and he's found!"*

*Joy is the inner celebration that nothing on the outside can change the fact that God loves me.*

## Joy Goes Beyond Happiness

*How wonderful that God wants us to go beyond the pursuit of happiness to experience joy. We can be joyful even when we're unhappy.*

All sorts of things can undermine happiness—time, change, and tragedy above all. There isn't anything intrinsically wrong with happiness, but trying to build on just the right set of circumstances is too insecure a base...

But the answer is not to reject happiness, it is to go beyond it, to joy.... Joy is different from happiness because of the cause of the ultimacy of its fulfillment and because it is a profound reality regardless of our circumstances. Rooted in God, empowered by the energies of the resurrection, joy does not depend on getting the right income, the perfect spouse, the right mix of things. Joy goes so far beyond happiness that it is present even in the midst of deep unhappiness.

REBECCA MANLEY PIPPERT, *HOPE HAS ITS REASONS* (1989)

## Joy From the Vine

*Many try to find joy in the fruit of the vine—wine. But true and lasting joy comes from the true vine—Jesus.*

Remember, in the first place, that the Vine was the Eastern symbol of Joy. It was its fruit that made glad the heart of man. Yet, however innocent that gladness—for the expressed juice of the grape was the common drink at every peasant's board—the gladness was only a gross and passing thing. This was not true happiness, and the vine of the Palestine vineyards was not the true vine. "*Christ* was the *true* Vine." Here, then, is the ultimate source of Joy. Through whatever media it reaches us, all true Joy and Gladness find their source in Christ.

HENRY DRUMMOND, *THE GREATEST THING IN THE WORLD* (1891)

## Happiness and Joy

*We all want to be happy, but joy goes much deeper. Joy is not based on circumstances or feelings, which change like the weather. True joy comes from a celebration of the heart over the things that do not change—things that come from God.*

The desire of happiness, beyond all doubt, is a natural desire. It is the law of life itself that every being seeks and strives toward the perfection of its kind, the realization of its own specific idea in form and function, and a true harmony with its environment. Every drop of sap in the tree flows toward foliage and fruit. Every drop of blood in the bird beats toward flight and song. In a conscious being this movement toward perfection must take a conscious form. This conscious form is happiness,—the satisfaction of the vital impulse,—the rhythm of the inward life,—the melody of a heart that has found its keynote. To say that all men long for this is simply to confess that all men are human, and that their thoughts and feelings are an essential part of their life. Virtue means a completed manhood. The joyful welfare of the soul belongs to the fulness of that ideal. Holiness is wholeness. In striving to realize the true aim of our being, we find the wish for happiness implanted in the very heart of our effort....

Men are not wrong in wishing for happiness, but wrong in their way of seeking it. *Earthly happiness*,—pleasure that belongs to the senses and perishes with them,— earthly happiness is a dream and a delusion. But *happiness on earth*,—spiritual joy and peace, blossoming here, fruiting hereafter,—immortal happiness, is the keynote of life in Christ.

And if we come to Him, He tells us four great secrets in regard to it.

i. It is inward, and not outward; and so it does not depend on what we have, but on what we are.

ii. It cannot be found by direct seeking, but by setting our faces toward the things from which it flows; and so we must climb the mount if we would see the vision, we must tune the instrument if we would hear the music.

iii. It is not solitary, but social; and so we can never have it without sharing it with others.

iv. It is the result of God's will for us, and not of our will for ourselves; and so we can only find it by giving our lives up, in submission and obedience, to the control of God....

This is the divine doctrine of happiness as Christ taught by His life and with His lips. If we want to put it into a single phrase, I know not where we shall find a more perfect utterance than in the words which have been taught us in childhood,—words so strong, so noble, so cheerful, that they summon the heart of manhood like marching music: "Man's chief end is to glorify God and enjoy Him forever."

HENRY VAN DYKE, *COUNSELS BY THE WAY* (1897)

## Open Up to Joy

*We miss so much joy just because we don't open ourselves up to all there is to enjoy. We can choose to embrace all the joy that today has to bring.*

There are joys which long to be ours. God sends ten thousand truths, which come about us like birds seeking inlet; but we are shut up to them, and so they bring us nothing, but sit and sing a while upon the roof and then fly away.

HENRY WARD BEECHER, *LIFE THOUGHTS* (1858)

## Prayer for Joy

*Pressures in our lives can crowd out the joy. Let's remember to pray and ask God to help us discover renewed joy.*

Lord God, I am not always thankful enough that I am a Christian. When I stop to think of all the blessings that come to me because I believe in You, I can only say that Your love for me is the greatest thing that has ever happened to me. Make me properly thankful for Your love, and let me never fail to be happy about it.

Help me to find real joy in worshiping You in church. Help me to sing the truths of the wonderful hymns with my heart as well as my lips. What I hear with my ear, send down deep into my heart. Let the joy of belonging to Jesus show itself in my words and actions, and make me a blessing to my family and friends.

Help me to share my joy of salvation with others. So many people are discouraged and disappointed over both little and large matters. Help me to say and do the right thing at the right time, that my friends may also find their happiness in Jesus on earth and joy with Him in heaven. Bless me in this for Jesus' sake. Amen.

*Teenagers Pray* (1955)

## The Joy of Discovery

*When we discover the treasures of life, joy follows. The birth of a baby, meeting with a wonderful friend, a long-awaited opportunity opened, a fresh look at the love of God—all these things stir our hearts to rejoice. But just imagine the joy at discovering how to use language—how to communicate. Helen Keller shares the joy of this exciting discovery in her life.*

We walked down the path to the well-house, attracted by the fragrance of the honeysuckle with which it was covered. Someone was drawing water and my teacher placed my hand under the spout. As the cool stream gushed over one hand she spelled into the other the word *water*, first slowly, then rapidly. I stood still, my whole attention fixed upon the motions of her fingers. Suddenly I felt a misty consciousness as of something forgotten—a thrill of returning thought; and somehow the mystery of language was revealed to me. I knew then that "w-a-t-e-r" meant the wonderful cool something that was flowing over my hand. That living word awakened my soul, gave it light, hope, joy, set it free! There were barriers still, it is true, but barriers that could in time be swept away.

I left the house eager to learn. Everything had a name, and each name gave birth to a new thought. As we returned to the house every object which I touched seemed to quiver with life. That was because I saw everything with the strange, new sight that had come to me. On entering the door I remembered the doll I had broken. I felt my way to the hearth and picked up the pieces. I had tried vainly to put them together. Then my eyes filled with tears; for I realized what I had done, and for the first time I felt repentance and sorrow.

I learned a great many new words that day. I do not remember what they all were; but I do know that *mother, father, sister, teacher* were among them—words that were to make the world blossom for me, "like Aaron's rod with flowers." It would have been difficult to find a happier child than I was as I lay in my crib at the close of that eventful day and lived over the joys it had brought me, and for the first time I longed for a new day to come.

HELEN KELLER, *THE STORY OF MY LIFE*

## The Flow of Joy

Sometimes I demand,
"God give me joy!"
and nothing happens.
Yet joy flows naturally,
lavishly,
when I seek to
know Him,
love Him, and
serve Him.

*Your joy comes from what you give, not from what you accumulate.*

FRANK C. LAUBACH, *PRAYER: THE MIGHTIEST FORCE IN THE WORLD* (1946)

*In Your presence is fullness of joy; At Your right hand are pleasures forevermore.*

PSALM 16:11 (NKJV), *HOLY BIBLE*